7 *Ingredients To An Effective Prayer Life*

7 Ingredients To An Effective Prayer Life

COMPILED BY
Trena D Stephenson

PUBLISHER
Daughters of Distinction

7 Ingredients To An Effective Prayer Life
Published by Daughters of Distinction
PO Box 9001
Silver Spring, Maryland 20906

Cover Design and Layout: Rever Designs & Yefim Kligerman
Editorial: Cynthia D. Thomas

ACKNOWLEDGEMENTS

With Many Thanks

First and foremost, I would like to thank God for being my creator and my all and all. To my beautiful daughter who I love dearly, thanks for the love and support you give continually. To my parents, my aunt Pastor Regina Holmes and my extended family thanks for being there when I needed you the most. To WofGod Inc. Staff and Affiliates thanks, so much for all you do to hold my arms up I couldn't do what I do without you. To my Daughters of Distinction staff you all rock! Thanks for all you do now we can breathe a little, don't get too comfortable though the ride is just beginning. To my Apostle James Tilghman and Senior Pastor Prophetess Greta Tilghman of Holy Temple Holiness Church of Deliverance, thanks for being such an awesome covering for me and my ministry team. I love you so very much. To the two awesome vessels of God who did the forward and review of this book, Prophetess Lucinda White, Firebrands for Christ Ministries, International and Prophetess Mia Grice-McGee, W.A.V.E Ministries, your contribution to this project is so appreciated. Last, but not least, thanks to all the co-authors of this book, I am so Godly proud of you the best is yet to come for each and every one of you. God stretched us and made us better vessels of honor for HIM. If I have forgotten anyone, Charge to my head and not my heart. Thank you, thank you, thank you.

With Love,
Trena

FOREWORD

Pastor Lucinda White - "The Woods Lady"

Some decades ago, I earnestly desired a holy and pure walk with God. I wanted intimacy, fellowship with God, and to be used by Him. I spent over fifteen years praying in the woods. This is the place where I deeply got to know Him. God ignited my fire in the woods and I became known to many as "The Woods Lady." While sitting and meditating upon how good God is, I realized that it was time for the church, even the entire nations, to return to the altar of God. In order to have an effective prayer life, our spirits must revert to a place of humility and submission. The scriptures tells us in 2 Chronicles 7:14, that as God's children, we should humble ourselves, pray, seek God's face and turn from our wicked ways; then God would hear us from heaven, forgive our sins, and heal our land.

Our God is concerned about restoring things back to Him for this intended purpose. Once upon a time, we were a people that lived for all night shut-ins, prayer meetings, consecrations, and just seeking the face of God. We were persistent, consistent, and determined to press continually until we shook and opened the heavens; as long as we were operative in these, we received desired results.

A prepared meal or dish has many ingredients that go into it. An ingredient is a component or element of something. It is any of the foods or substances that are combined to make a particular dish or meal. For instance, to bake a cake, some of the basic ingredients needed are butter; eggs, flour, sugar, flavoring, and milk; if any of these are missing the dish then become ineffective.

In other words, your cake will be undesirable. An effective prayer life consists of repentance, humility, submission, and sanctification. It is the effectual fervent prayer of the righteous man that avails much. The book of James talks about the Prophet Elisha, who was subject to like passions as we are. He prayed that it would not rain upon the earth, and the rain was withheld for three and one half years. When he desired rain, he prayed again, the heaven yielded rain, and the earth brought forth fruit.

Therefore, Elisha was successful and effective in his prayer life producing desired results. <u>Seven Ingredients to An Effective Prayer Life</u> is a book, which imparts humility and wisdom on how to seek God's face. In this book, you will read testimonies of various authors that will propel your spirit into another dimension in seeking God. The transparent and heartfelt words will cause faith to come alive and provoke a stirring in one's soul.

Prophetess Lucinda White
Founder of Lucinda White Ministries (LWM)
Co-Pastor Firebrands For Christ Ministries, Int'l (FFC)
603 Abbott Street Linden, AL 36748
www.lucindawhite.org

PREFACE

When an individual speaks of prayer, many definitions may come to mind. However, the true meaning can be defined as communicating with God. In order for prayer to be effective there must be 2-way communication, meaning that you cannot do all the talking, there must be some listening on your part to the receiver of your petition, which is God.

In this book, you will find testimonials of individuals that have learned that "traditional" praying is not enough. It has to go further; one must have an effective prayer life. According to dictionary.com, effective is defined as adequate to accomplish a purpose; producing the intended or expected result. So, if this is not what is taking place in your prayer life, you will find within these pages ingredients that can lead you into an effective prayer life. You may ask this question, "Why will it only lead me and not give me an effective prayer life?" Great question, the logic or reasoning behind this is because you are going to get out of this process what you put in. There is no sure way that anyone can tell you an absolute way to achieve an effective prayer life. However, this book serves as a tool or resource to assist you in your relationship with the Lord in the areas of prayer. As you turn the pages of this book, you will find yourself within some of the content and then will be able to grow closer to God by the wisdom, knowledge, and understanding that came from these willing vessels of God. As I reviewed this book, the words that come from these pages have gave me an even closer look at my very own relationship and prayer life with God.

In closing, now it is your turn to experience this life-changing journey into the Seven Ingredients to an Effective Prayer Life. The compiler, as well as the co- authors of this book, did an excellent job in providing relevant testimonials and biblical principles of what it takes to achieve an effective prayer life. Realizing that this cannot be done overnight, however with dedication and commitment it can provide great success. I would exhort you to pay attention to the first two ingredients featured and allow your spiritual taste buds to recognize every detailed morsel. Then dive in and enjoy this awesome dish of a book with the richness of the word and the pure taste of God entitled Seven Ingredients to An Effective Prayer Life (Volumes 1 & 2). In addition, stay tuned more volumes with more ingredients to follow this one. I bid unto you great reading and blessings!

Prophetess Mia Grice-McGee
Overseer of W.A.V.E. Ministries
www.miamcgee.org

VOLUME ONE - HUMILITY

TABLE OF CONTENTS

VOLUME 1 HUMILITY

CHAPTER 1

A Heart of Repentance

Before we talk about what humility is, let me tell you what it is not! Humility is not about a lowly look or demeanor. It is not about a plain dowdy dress code, nor is it about a soft- spoken individual or a loud one for that matter. I think you can surmise here that humility is not about the outward appearance, but it's about the heart. *"The sacrifices of God are a broken spirit: a broken and a contrite heart, O God, thou wilt not despise."*(Psalm 51:17 King James Version KJV). When we come before the Lord in prayer, the first thing we should do is come with a heart of repentance. Repent for what you may ask. You may think, but I haven't done anything. Ok, so you must be dead then! Although we may not recall anything specific that we have said or done, nine times out of ten we have offended someone. Since we don't want anything hindering our prayers, it is always good to begin by asking for forgiveness. Do we want to be effective in our prayer life or mince words about whether or not we've done something for which we must ask forgiveness? *"And forgive us our debts, as we forgive our debtors."* (Matthew 6:12 KJV). When we pray, it is always in order to ask for forgiveness for our trespasses.

What Is Humility All About?

Humility is all about depending totally on the Lord, maintaining that dependency, as well as obeying Him at any cost. Humility is defined as a lack of false pride. The opposite of false is true. Let us all strive for a lack of false pride. When we are humble, we know that in our flesh, we don't measure up, but we also know who we are in Christ. It is imperative that we always remember that everything that's accomplished in our life is only by the grace of God. Another way to put it is to say that our ultimate dependency is upon Him. It's alright to acknowledge the gifts He has blessed you with or how else would you hone them and nurture them? However, we still have to be cognizant that we cannot do anything in our flesh, but rather everything should be done by His power in order to be effective. Our mere effectiveness comes by His power and by His spirit not by our flesh. *"Then he answered and spake unto me, saying, This is the word of the Lord unto Zerubbabel, saying, Not by might, nor by power, but by my spirit, saith the Lord of hosts."* (Zechariah 4:6 KJV).

Maintaining Dependency on the Lord

What keeps me humble is remembering with heartfelt gratitude what the Lord has done for me. I am ever conscious that I literally can do nothing without Him! It's one thing to make that statement, but a completely different thing to know it. My mind goes back to my childhood days when I didn't have many of the things I needed. I was extremely bothered by it back then, but now I appreciate the humble beginnings because it taught me total dependency on Him. It was a reality that I truly needed the Lord in every area of my life. During my childhood, I had to depend on God because there was no one else to depend on, but now I want to depend on Him. Since I literally came to Him as a child, He always answered my prayer. I might add that He didn't always answer the way I thought He should have, but He did respond.

Now that I am an adult, and have matured in the Lord, I still come to Him as a child. We can never say it enough! The Lord loves it when we come to Him as a child telling Him how much we need Him. There is a chorus (refrain) of a song that comes to mind written by Annie Hawks, "I Need Thee Every Hour."[1]

I need thee oh I need thee
Every hour I need thee
Oh, bless me now my savior
I come to thee

Obedience is Better

"And Samuel said, Hath the Lord as great delight in burnt offerings and sacrifices, as in obeying the voice of the Lord? Behold, to obey is better than sacrifice, and to hearken than the fat of rams."(I Samuel 15:22 KJV).

When you go to God in prayer with humility and a child-like attitude, He will talk back to you. He will give you specific instructions. Why is this? Because He knows, you were sincere. You followed His prescribed method. Now the question is – "Will you obey His voice?" Shirley Caesar sings the following words in the song "Yes Lord, Yes."[2]

I'll say yes Lord, yes
To your will and to your way
I'll say yes Lord yes
I will trust you and obey

And when the Spirit speaks to me
With my whole heart I'll agree
And my answer will be yes, Lord, yes.

There you have it! No matter what it is, whether you want to or not, your answer should be yes Lord, yes. Behold to obey is much better than any trumped up sacrifice you could ever bring to Him. Nothing pleases God, but what He asked for. Why would you insult Him by doing something He didn't ask for? Go ahead and do what God told you to do. Do it now!

Lack of Humility

When we are lacking humility, four major things creep into our lives pride, haughtiness, selfishness, and dishonor. Let's talk about pride. *"The fear of the LORD is to hate evil: pride, and arrogancy, and the evil way, and the froward mouth, do I hate."* (Proverbs 8:13 KJV). The lack of humility will cause us to be puffed up in pride, which the Lord hates.

Pride

When we are praying to the Father and we are steeped in pride, the Lord knows it. He knows that we really feel like we can handle our own problems because we are grown, we have the education, the finances, etc. In all honesty, we're just saying prayers. Saying prayers and connecting with the Father are two different things. When God knows that we're speaking directly to Him with sincere anticipation and expectation, He answers us because as I've said before, He knows we're depending on Him. *"When I was a child, I spake as a child; I understood as a child, I thought as a child:*

but hen I became a man, I put away childish things." (I Corinthians 13:11 KJV). Yes, I realize that you have put away childless things, but we must always maintain a child-like attitude where God is concerned. A child-like attitude is one of total dependency upon our Father.

Haughtiness

"Pride goeth before destruction, and an haughty spirit before a fall." (Proverbs 16:18 KJV). If you're looking for a prescription for a fall, take a dose of haughtiness and call me in the morning!

It amazes me that, no matter how many times we see someone fall due to a haughty spirit, we get caught up in that same snare. God's instructions to keep us from a spirit of haughtiness are plain and simple. *"For I say, through the grace given unto me, to every man that is among you, not to think of himself more highly than he ought to think; but to think soberly, according as God hath dealt to every man the measure of faith."* (Romans 12:3 KJV).

Selfishness

Means you're only concerned for your own welfare and a disregard of others. When we go to God in prayer, we don't go begging God for this, that and the other for ourselves.

I am a firm believer that when you pray for others, God will have someone pray for you.

Dishonor

A lack of humility causes us to dishonor God by saying: I really don't believe that you're the one performing these miracles in my life. These things are done because I have the credentials.

The truth is I don't really need your help because I got this.

I am just coming to you as a form of Godliness. What is a form of Godliness? The form of Godliness is asking for God's help, yet ignoring His help when He sends it. *"Having a form of godliness, but denying the power thereof: from such turn away."* (II Timothy 3:5 KJV).

This is false humility because it dishonors God. It dishonors Him because as soon as He starts to respond to our request, and He's not answering the way we want, we ignore Him. This is something that can easily be remedied. Let's begin to listen intently in order to give in to His power to respond in the way He knows is best.

Benefits of Humility

The benefits of humility are innumerable. Three specific benefits are honor, riches, and life more abundantly.

Honor: It is one thing for you to honor God, but it is another thing for Him to honor you back. What does it mean for God to honor you? Well, it simply means that when you pray with humility, you have built up a two-way connection and that whatever you ask in His name in humility – He will do it.

In other words, the Lord will honor your request because whatever you're asking is for the up building of the kingdom of God. We've often heard that when we take care of God's business, He'll take care of ours." I have tried this and I know it works!

Riches: Another benefit of humility is riches. When we speak of riches, we immediately think of money. *"A feast is made for laughter, and wine maketh merry: but money answereth all things."* (Ecclesiastes 10:19 KJV). Money does not make you happy and it certainly does not put you in some kind of special place with Him because you have it. In other words, riches consist of so much more than money. We can be rich due to the kind of family and friends the Lord has blessed us with. Being rich can also consist of relationships the Lord has enabled us to develop and maintain. More importantly, we can be rich with the favor of God. My husband often says, "Favor can take you where money can't."

Abundant Life: Abundant life is automatic when you are clothed in humility and the grace of God follows you. *"You younger men, likewise, be subject to your elders; and all of you, clothe yourselves with humility toward one another, for God is opposed to the proud, but gives grace to the humble."* (I Peter 5:5 New American Standard Bible NAS). In order to walk in humility we must wear it as a garment. Most people think class has to do with designer clothing, the kind of car you drive, where you live, etc. Class has little to do with any of those things. Class is from the inside out.

It is how you show respect and dignity to every individual simply because they're a human being and not because of their status. Wearing humility is from the inside out as well and when you possess it, you have the abundant life. *"The thief cometh not, but for to steal, and to kill, and to destroy: I am come that they might have life, and that they might have it more abundantly."* (John 10:10 KJV).

The Decision and Greatest Benefit of Humility:

The decision to humble yourself is yours, for the word tells us to *"Humble yourselves therefore under the mighty hand of God, that He may exalt you in due time."* (I Peter 5:6 KJV). Humbling yourself is total submission under God's hand. So if you're choosing to humble yourself under the mighty hand of God. He's getting ready to exalt you in due time. There is a phrase that the Lord gave me some years ago that says, "I know in my knower" (since then I've heard others use it) -- that most of you reading this chapter are getting ready to be exalted. Another way of putting it is "get ready for your next promotion."

The benefit of your decision to humble yourself is priceless for *"Whosoever therefore shall humble himself as this little child, the same is greatest in the kingdom of heaven."* (Matthew 18:4 KJV). Be the greatest, maintain a heart of repentance, and choose to humble yourself!

Let us pray! Father in the name of Jesus, we repent of every thought, word, or deed that we have committed today. We appreciate your love, kindness, and patience with us. Our desire is to hear and obey your voice. We come as a child in a spirit of humility, for you are our Father in deed. Our deepest desire is to please you in all things. Amen.

DR. PRISCILLA PENN

Pastor Priscilla Penn is a respected prophetic voice, prolific teacher, prayer warrior, worship specialist, and lover of God. She serves as a "living epistle" actively spreading the Gospel of Jesus Christ in a way that produces change in the lives of everyone she meets. Dr. Penn has partnered with many ministries, Christian leaders, and business persons for more than 20 years to equip and empower individuals to maximize their potential. Her extraordinary presentation of the gospel makes her a highly sought after preacher, teacher, counselor, and spiritual mother.

In 1992, she received her call to ministry and began ministerial training at Greater Morning Star in Washington, D.C. In 1995, under the leadership of Dr. Phyllis P. Heath of Bethesda Temple Apostolic Church , she attended Aenon Bible College and became a licensed minister of the Pentecostal Assemblies of the World, Inc. Dr. Penn earned her Ph.D. in Religious Philosophy from Tabernacle Bible College and Seminary, Tampa , FL in 2007. She and her husband of 42 years, Dr. Timothy Penn founded Owrah Fellowship Ministries

(OFM) in 1999, currently in Warrenton, VA. In October 2011, Priscilla and her husband were ordained pastors into Mount Olive Kingdom Fellowship Covenant Ministries with Presiding Prelate Bishop Dr. Shirley Holloway.

Pastor Penn is the committed mother of two daughters, later adopting a third daughter. She also has one son-in-love, two grandchildren, and a host of spiritual sons and daughters.

Dr. Penn is convinced that everything she has gone through in life was designed to prepare her for the work that God has called her to do. Truly, she is a leader of leaders often sought after by apostles and pastors to navigate the various stages of life and ministry. Having a keen ear and a heart for obeying the voice of God, Dr. Penn has the ability to speak into the lives of others allowing them to embrace and experience God. She has given her life to instructing, equipping, loving, and empowering individuals to pursue the plan of God for their lives. She is one of God's trusted vessels, charged to minister the uncompromising Word of God with passion and love.

www.owrah.com

CHAPTER 2

The Posture of an Intercessors Prayer life: What Is Your Position

Humility[3]-the quality or condition of being humble; meekness, and submissiveness

When I think of the word humility, the three things that come to mind are humbleness, suffering, and helplessness. Humbleness takes us to a place where we can do nothing, but totally depend on God. We become humbled at our lowest moment, whether it's the loss of a job, finances being out of order or a bad report from the doctor.

Suffering brings us to the point of seeking God in our sickness, mental health, marital issues or loss of a loved one. We are helpless because of things we put ourselves through and then we turn to our Father to get us out of our mess.

Therefore, in that, we go to the Father in prayer with a sincere heart crying out for help. This is because sometimes we struggle with things of the flesh. Within this struggle, we suffer with unforgiveness in our hearts from those who have hurt and persecuted us. It seems as though we can't get past the hurt of past relationships, family mem bers, the church as well as friends. Sometimes as Christians, we find ourselves asking questions as to why do we have to be the bigger person? Or why do we have to be the ones to forgive?

The answer to the above questions, are simple. It is because we are the body of Christ, and have to live by the scriptures, which are His commandments and His instructions. It does not matter who is at fault or what you have done. What matters is getting it right. Christ also found Himself in a humbled position, when He went through the transition of being crucified. He appeared helpless, because it was His own people who denied and crucified Him.

When we humble ourselves, it allows God to get to the heart of the matter. You see God deals with the hearts of His people because He knows His children so well. He knows when we are hurting, when we are disobedient as well as when we are in sin.

The one thing I do know is that He allows us to come to Him in prayer to cast all of our cares upon Him. He wants us to lay at His feet at all times. Why does it take humility to do what God asks of us? How many times does He have to give us instructions before we act on it? Are we not tired of being beat down? Why do we run? I had to ask myself these questions many times and always came up with the same answer, "FEAR."

Why are we in fear? God said that He would take care of us. What is the difference in having faith as small as a mustard seed while living in a world of sin, and having the same faith, which we lack in the body of Christ? Is it so hard to walk in the anointing that He has placed on our lives?

In some ways as children in the body of Christ, we appear to be no different than the world. Yes, we should be different, but are we really that different? There are some of us who still think and act like the world and come to church as if nothing is going on, while kneeling at the altar praying repetitious prayers.

God is getting tired of the same prayers day after day, night after night. He wants that connection, that relationship which is only between you and Him. You see, praying in the spirit allows us to have an affectionate relationship with Him. It is the type of relationship, where you never want to leave His presence.

It's the type of prayer that consumes you. You are so drunk in the spirit you just want to stay right there. The best part is the enemy is not allowed to enter in. When we pray aloud, the enemy takes every word that we say and use it to his advantage. That's why we have to learn how to flip the script on him and change our way of praying. As I always say, we have to learn how to confuse the enemy.

"Likewise, ye younger, submit yourselves unto the elder. Yea, all of you be subject one to another, and be clothed with humility: for God resisteth the proud, and giveth grace to the humble. Humble yourselves therefore under the mighty hand of God, that he may exalt you in due time: Casting all your cares upon him; for he careth for you." (I Peter 5:5-7 KJV).

Peter tells us that we have to submit ourselves one to another. As I began to read this scripture, I looked back over my life during the time I was married to my husband of 18 years, who is now deceased. Not only was it an abusive relationship, but my husband was also a drug addict. It was because of the drugs our marriage was always in turmoil.

I remember going to one of my husband's addiction meetings because I wanted to be involved with his recovery. When I was told by his counselor, that I had to take him back after everything he had done to me, I looked at the counselor as if she were crazy and then cussed. Yes, I said "cussed." The crazy part was he was still my husband. Although the book of Ephesians 5:22 (KJV), states, "*Wives submit to your husbands,*" I was nowhere in the submission mode. And of course, to tell you the truth I was still in my backsliding stages.

Additionally, a caseworker at the Department of Social Services informed me that because he was HIV positive, I had to take care of him. I really looked at them like they were crazy and cussed because they told me that my finances were enough to take care of me, him and two children. But, he was still my husband. What I am saying, because God knew my heart and although I said I was not going to do what they asked, I had to humble myself to a situation I had no control over. Nevertheless, today I can say that although my husband went home to be with the Lord, I was obedient in doing what I was supposed to do. I fasted and prayed even in my situation.

My situation reminded me, of how God told Hosea to "*Take unto him a wife of whoredom.*" (Hosea 1:1-11 KJV). Because of his faithfulness unto the Lord, Hosea married Gomer and he became humble to his situation. While Gomer continued in her lifestyle as well as birth three children, Hosea continued to do the will of the Lord. And although Hosea may not have understood, there was purpose in what God was doing. God will put us in a position just to see how we will handle it. We become humbled because we just want to please Him. We have to understand that whenever God place us in any positions, there is a purpose in it to make, mold and move us into our destiny. When Peter talked about submitting one to another, he was also talking to the church as well. You find there are a lot of Christians who don't do well under authority. Instead of following instructions, they rebel doing things their own way. It's really ironic how there are so many religious people, yes that's right "religious" in the house of God who rather continue to live in sin, instead of humbling themselves before that brother or sister admitting that they were wrong. Humbling ourselves in humility means learning how to talk to one another as well as, being respectful of those who have authority over us. The bible tells us to love one another as God loved us. Is being angry with someone worth more than your soul and forgiving others?

"But I say unto you, Love your enemies, bless them that curse you, do good to them that hate you, and pray for them which despitefully use you, and persecute you. That ye may be the children of your Father which is in heaven: for he maketh his sun to rise on the evil and on the good, and sendeth rain on the just and on the unjust." (Matthew 5:44-45 KJV). God is telling us to love those who wrong us. How can we do this, without being humiliated knowing that we have to bring our flesh under subjection, to pray even when we don't want to. Also, having to chalk it up with a smile and love them in spite of everything they do. Knowing if we had our way it would not be done.

There are times, I find myself praying never hearing the voice of God. I become frustrated because I don't know what to do in some of my situations. The point we have to realize, God is waiting on us to do the things we need to do, to get it right.

The problem is we expect for Him to do everything for us. Although He can solve all of our problems, we have to meet Him part of the way, as well.

In the year of 2001, I made the decision to move to Aberdeen, MD with my two younger children not knowing that my life would drastically change. It was a time when everything was chaotic because of the situation with the World Trade Center and things were going crazy. It was also at that time, I decided that I had to make a change in my life for the better. I began packing and two weeks after the World Trade Center's incident, and the day of a plane crash in Queens N.Y., I was on the road to a new beginning. I asked God if I had made the right decision but, I do not think He ever answered me. And I did not know if it was the right thing to do or maybe He did answer me, and I wasn't really hearing Him, or did not recognize His true voice.

At that time, I didn't know if I was running away from the issues of dealing with my family, or if God had a strategic plan for my life that I didn't know about. Also at that time, my husband was in the hospital due to his illness and was unable to make the move to Maryland with us. As I settled down in Aberdeen, I traveled back and forth every weekend to visit my husband until he went home to be with the Lord on February 19, 2002.

My children and I resided in the home of my nephew and his wife. My sister also lived in the home as well with her husband. It was a very complicated situation. Even with a four- year degree, I could not find a job and everywhere I went, I was told, I was over qualified.

Over qualified I really didn't understand it. I asked one of the po tential employers, to define what that meant. After living with my nephew for about three to six months, the rental office found out we were living there and everyone had to move because we were in breach of the lease.

At that point, my children and I became homeless and began living in hotels. I was very angry to be put in a situation like that because of being told that everything would be alright. I was so humbled and humiliated at that time, because I was never put in a position like that before.

To this day, my family never knew what happened because I never told them. But, even in that, I knew that God had me. Although my children wanted to move back to N.Y., there was something that held me from moving back home. My family was very upset that I made such a big move in the first place. I wanted to prove them wrong especially when they told me I didn't know what I was doing. It has been 12 years, since my move and I am still here. This is because God had a plan for my life. If I had moved back home, my destiny may not have been filled according to the will of God. What my family didn't know, is that God had plans for me.

When we don't believe and trust in God, it puts us in a state of humbleness as well. This is because once we are given a diagnosis of a bad report from the doctor we begin to worry. Knowing that God is a healer, we become double minded with fear setting in and we go to God with a humbled spirit seeking his help.

"If my people, which are called by my name, shall humble themselves, and pray, and seek my face, and turn from their wicked ways; then will I hear from heaven, and will forgive their sin, and will heal their land." (II Chronicles 7:14 KJV).

God is telling us that we must humble ourselves before Him in prayer at all times, not sometimes, but all times. Our insecurities of who we are, will always lead us away from God.

He has already put a mandate on our lives of who we are in Him and how we are to carry out His instructions pertaining to our lives. It is up to us to follow through with our assignments, not being afraid of people or making a mistake. There is no mistake in what God asks of us. We must do it with a humble spirit and not out of our flesh. For if we do it in our flesh, we will mess everything up. Humility is being humbled when praying for others who persecute you.

Humility is praying for people and God tells you to stop because they are out of His will and asking the Father to give them another chance. Humility is having the heart of the people when praying, feeling their hearts weeping uncontrollably for them. Humility is trying to bring your flesh under subjection from sin. Humility is feeling the heart of God to the point, where you can actually feel His hurt, and His pain. Humility is hearing the warnings and not taking heed to them. Humility is living in disobedience. Humility is making sure our prayers are effective.

My Prayer

Heavenly Father I pray as the people are reading this chapter, the fervent prayers of the righteous availeth much. You open up their eyes and reveal yourself to them so they can see you. Open their ears that they can hear you and penetrate their hearts to receive your word. I pray that the words in this chapter will open up their understanding of who you are. Father I also ask that they humble themselves before you in prayer, asking for forgiveness of their sins. In Jesus, name AMEN.

MINISTER THERESA LEWIS

Minister Lewis was born in Brooklyn, New York. She is the mother of four children (2) deceased and grandmother of four granddaughters. Minister Lewis attends Word of Faith International Outreach Ministries under the Leadership of Bishop Melvin T. Taylor and Prophetess Carol V. Taylor. She rededicated her life to the Lord in July 2002, and was baptized in the name of Jesus on October 5, 2002, during which she accepted the call on her life to the prophetic. She is a Prophetic Intercessor of Prayer and serves on Shepherd Care Ministry.

Minister Lewis is also, one of the authors of And He Still Speaks. Minister Lewis traveled to Port Au Prince and Dessalines Haiti with her pastor on numerous missionary trips. She continues to be on fire for the Lord pursuing her goals of evangelizing and winning souls for the kingdom.

CHAPTER 3

Like A Child, Humble in Spirit

"I tell you the truth, unless you change and become like little children, you will never enter the kingdom of Heaven. Therefore, whoever humbles himself like this child is the greatest in the Kingdom of Heaven." (Matthew 18: 3-4 New International Version NIV).

Take a moment and think back to your childhood. Do you remember how innocent and trusting you were? Or, how you often did what you were told to do? When we were children, we most likely accepted whatever those in authority over us said. We began to experience humility in our childhood state. Our hearts were humble. A humble heart realizes that it does not know everything. It understands that it does not yet hold all of the answers and, that it must seek direction before it ventures down the road of life. However, being humble in God does not mean that we are timid or lack confidence. It does not mean that we are undeserving or fearful. In fact, God's word teaches the opposite. As children of the Most High, we must have an innocent trust in God and know that our confidence is in Him (Psalm 71:5). We are certain that *we are deserving* of all good things (Psalm 84:11; Romans 8:28 & 32). And, we know that His perfect love casts out all fear (I John 4:18).

To be humble is a state of the spirit and mind. When we humble ourselves before God, we allow His thoughts about who we are to flourish within and around us. Therefore, do not allow your thoughts to exalt themselves against the knowledge of God who formed you (II Corinthians 10:5). Always, look to Him and your way will be made sure (Psalm 37:23). Become like a child, humble in spirit so you can enter into and see the Kingdom of God where everything is already provided. There is no need or lack there.

In the Garden of Eden before Adam & Eve came into agreement with the enemy's words, they experienced"thy kingdom come and thy will be done"right here on earth, where they were. Everything was provided and manifested in the natural for them to experience and enjoy.

However, when they listened to and entertained the thoughts of the enemy they questioned God's holy word. When we question God's word, we cease to be humble in our thoughts. God does not mind if we ask Him questions. However, I believe He does mind if we question whether He knows what is best and right for us. Adam and Eve allowed their thoughts to exalt itself above God's thoughts concerning them. At that point, they ceased to experience the Kingdom, which is a state of mind and spirit that ultimately becomes manifested in the physical realm. And thus, they saw lack of provision and protection and they became afraid.

They hid themselves and God came looking for them and said, "Where are you? They were no longer in the kingdom (In His will, where everything is provided). Adam gave evidence through his spoken word that he was no longer experiencing and seeing the kingdom, when he said that they were hiding because they were na-ked. And God's response was "Who told you that you were naked?" (Genesis 3:11 NIV). Beloved, God is asking us the same question now, when we are not experiencing the kingdom (of divine joy, peace, love, abundant provision, revelation, light, protection and health). Who told you that you were afraid, poor, sick, not loved or worthy of good things? I believe when God asks this question, it's a clue to check our thinking. What have you come into agreement with? Two cannot walk together unless they agree (Amos 3:3). When we get out of agreement with God's thoughts (His Word) concerning us, we align ourselves with the enemy of our souls and mind. We cease to be humble in spirit, like a child and therefore, cease to experience God's kingdom. His kingdom is always filled with His great love, joy, peace, provision, healing, and abundance of whatever you need. Remember, it is His will and good pleasure to give you the kingdom (Luke 12:32).

So check your thoughts against the word of God daily (bread) and come into agreement with it so you can enter & experience His kingdom and receive ALL that He has already provided! Amen!

Our thoughts become aligned with Gods thoughts through reading His word, which has the power to change our circumstances and us. Next step, declare who He says you are! Declare that you are experiencing (be detailed) ALL that you need, right here on earth. His word says YOU shall decree a thing and it shall be established/done (Job 22:28; Matthew 17:20; Mark 11:23). Declare and decree it in prayer!

Follow Jesus' Lead

One of the greatest pieces of wisdom, I can think of, is to find someone who has done something extremely well and follow their lead. This may surprise you, but when I think of humility, I think of Jesus! In the beginning was God (John 1:1). And God being our greatest example humbled Himself and wrapped Himself in flesh. He allowed Himself to be birthed, held and cared for by a woman He knew would love Him. Her name was Mary. Likewise, we must follow His example and humble ourselves to be birthed into His grace, be held by His Word and cared for by His great love for us. "For God so loved the world (that means you) that He gave His only begotten son (Jesus), that whosoever (that means you) would believe on Him shall be saved (John 3:16 KJV)." That's where we begin, if you have not already asked (prayed) and received God's extended arm of grace, His forgiveness, His acceptance of you through salvation, I invite you to do so now. That's our beginning, finding our way back to God, our loving Heavenly Father.

So, what do we do now that we are saved by grace? How do we pray after we've had our beginning in Him? I suggest we follow His lead and think, believe, and pray like He prayed!

How to Pray

Jesus told us how to pray. And every time Jesus prayed, miracles happened! So, it would be beneficial to look at how Jesus prayed. Let's look at Matthew 6:9-13. He starts His prayer by proclaiming who He is talking to "Our Father who art in Heaven." This instructs us to acknowledge Him as our Father. Now before we move on with the prayer, it's imperative that we don't leap over too lightly the *Our Father* part. I believe that God wants you to know whom you are approaching. You are approaching and coming before *your Father.* I don't know what your earthly example of a father has been. Your earthly father may have been loving, or mean to the bone. You may have known him, or he may have been absent from your life. Whatever the situation, God wants you to know that you are not approaching that earthly father who is at best, imperfect. You are approaching your Heavenly Father who is PERFECT. You are approaching *LOVE.* The bible tells us that God is love (1 John 4: 8).

Think about it for a moment, when we know that we are in the presence of someone that really loves us, we know that we can be comfortable, we know that we can be at peace, we know that we can probably have what we ask. And so it is when we approach our Loving Heavenly Father, we know that we are approaching love. We can be certain that it is our Loving Heavenly Father's good pleasure to give us the kingdom (Luke 12:31-32).

Because He is from everlasting to everlasting, because He is the King of Kings and Lord of Lords, we should praise Him. But, if that's not enough to get your heart filled with praise, just concentrate for a moment on the following: Are you alive? Do you have movement of at least one of your limbs? Do you have the ability to think? Has God ever done anything for you? If so, then you have cause to praise Him! Jesus said, "Hallowed be thy name!" Here, He is counseling, urging us to praise our God. Even if things are going seemingly wrong and confusion seems to be all around, don't despair. Start to praise the Lord. I believe that Jesus is teaching us this because He knows that praise is a weapon of the spirit that the enemy can't stand and furthermore, can't win against.

When you begin praising God, know that you're about to

Daughters of Distinction

enter the atmosphere where miracles happen. Remember we are following Jesus' lead and this is how He prayed. And when Jesus prayed, miracles happened! When you pray miracles _can_ happen. Jesus continued the prayer by instructing us to declare that His Kingdom come! Where? Here, on earth where you are, where your situation is.He then declared "Thy will be done!" Here Jesus is leading us to do the same. You have to declare that God's will shall be done! Where? Here on earth where you are, where your situation is. How? Declare His will be done here, where you are just like it is in Heaven.

Child of God, I declare unto you that _anything_ you need is already provided, any problem you have, the answer is already worked out…if you believe (Matthew 9:23).

Jesus tells you in no uncertain terms that you should ask of the Father for your daily bread. He used the word daily. Hmm, I wonder why? It's because He is instructing us to come boldly before your loving Heavenly Father every day. Every day He urges us to come back and get filled with His presence, refreshed with His great love for us, get refocused on the fact that you are an overcomer, a victor and not a victim!

He tells us to forgive, oh my, that's a big one. You mean I have to forgive the one who abused me, who raped me, who spoke lies against me, the one who stole from me or who told me that I would never amount to anything? The answer, beloved, is yes! Why, you may be thinking? It's really simple because holding on to unforgiveness keeps you seeing yourself as a victim. Remember, we have to humble ourselves and think the thoughts that God thinks about us. God says we are victors not victims! It's your choice, it's your decision how you want to see yourself, and how you want to be seen.

If you want to see the kingdom, you will have to humble yourself and ensure your thoughts do not exalt themselves above God's thoughts about you! And yes, it is a temptation to hold on to the unforgiveness. So, ask God to release you or deliver you from that temptation. Why? Because you need to be free. I declare unto you that this is your year of freedom, if you will choose to humble yourself and think of yourself and see yourself as God, your Loving Heavenly Father sees you. Amen!

May I inspire you to get in to the HIGH Praise…because it is there, in the high praise that we enter into the atmosphere where all miracles exist all day long! What we call a miracle, God calls an everyday experience! Enter into that atmosphere, where our Father's love can reach us, where there is no lack, where miracles happen, where our hope is renewed. Let's approach LOVE and receive GRACE and God's FAVOR!

Let Us Pray

Our Loving Heavenly Father who art in Heaven, we praise your name. We praise and thank you for how great your love is for us. We thank you that we have no lack, but rather an abundance of *your* love surrounding us and filling us until we overflow with it. We thank you that you are the beginning and the end and everything in between. We thank you that you hold us, with confidence in the palm of your mighty hand (Isaiah 49:16). We declare right now that your Kingdom come, right here where we are (in our situation) and we declare that *your will* be done just as *your will is* done in Heaven! We thank you that it is *your* good pleasure to give us on a daily basis our portion of bread. Jesus said "I am the bread of life" in John 6:48

(KJV). We thank you that we are delivered from the temptation to hold on to unforgiveness because we realize that it causes us to see ourselves differently then you see us. We thank you for your spirit of humility and that we may trust you as innocent children do. We thank you that we are victors in you (1 John 5:4)! We forgive because we understand that unforgiveness is just a cheap trick of the enemy to try to keep us bound up. But, we declare that this is our year of freedom and we will walk in it now and forevermore. Father, as victorious ones and as children who were made in your image and in your likeness, just as you spoke and things were we speak into our day the following:

I am the righteousness of God and I am surrounded by my Heavenly Father's good will for me. I declare and decree that His Kingdom has come, and that His will is being done right here where I am. I speak into this day the light of God and the clarity of God's word. I thank you that you are illuminating all that I need to see. I declare that His Holy angels are encamped all around my family, friends, the entire Body of Christ and me. I declare that the earth is full of His goodness and His goodness is being made manifest unto me and before me this day. I declare that this is the day that the Lord has made and I have already made up my mind to be glad and rejoice in it! I speak into this day that I have more than enough and that everything I need is provided and manifested before me. I declare that your love, your way, and your will are illuminated before me this day. I speak into this day the love of God full and running over to others that I meet and greet. I speak into this day the fullness of God, my loving Father! In Jesus name, Amen!

MINISTER PAMELA JOHNSON-HOOD

Pamela is a native of Southern California. She now resides in Virginia with her loving husband and four children. Pamela is a veteran of the United States Military, having served honorably both stateside and overseas. She is a graduate of Yale University and is currently completing her Doctorate degree in Clinical Psychology. She serves as a group counselor for women in distress.

Additionally, she is a minister in development and serves as an integral member of the intercessory and altar team for the Sisters of the Son Ministry in Spotsylvania, Virginia. She is often called upon to give mental health speeches within the community, and to minister to women at Women's day programs. Love is her motive, as she points others toward their highest good while teaching them about their true identity and value in Christ. Her passion for Christ is contagious…Catch it!

CHAPTER 4

Tragedy to Purpose

Have you ever experienced a devastating life tragedy, one that immediately brought you to your knees? A tragedy that completely shattered whom you once thought you were. Christians have this remarkable ability of smiling and greeting one another with the words "praise the Lord or God is good all the time," even in the mist of personal trials. When tragedy knocks at your front door can, you still smile and speak the words praise the Lord? I was one of those Christians that had the ability to laugh and smile in the mist of any situation, and then life happened.

One beautiful sunny Labor Day weekend I was informed of the tragic death of my only child. After 19 amazing years, my son was killed following his first year of college. Once I received the news, my life completely changed forever. My flesh proceeded to die at such a rapid pace I could hardly feel myself breath. The heaviness now living in my chest felt like someone had placed a large boulder there; the pain was more than I could bear. My heart was no longer whole; the center was missing as if someone had taken a double barrel shotgun and proceeded to release devastating bullets through it. What was left of my heart was just fluttering from the constant pain.

Completely crushed by the words Andrae was shot, and he did not make it. Living through this tragedy was the most humbling experience because I could no longer hide behind the laughter and constant smiles. Finally, the mask was removed and my facial expression was shattered. Spiritual brokenness brought me to a place of desperation, totally dependent on God for every aspect of my life.

"The Lord is near to those who have a broken heart, and saves such as have a contrite spirit." (Psalms 34:18 New King James Version NKJV). According to Psalms 34:8, brokenness is a way to the heart of God. The process of brokenness is critical in building character and Christian maturity. When I think of the word brokenness, I am reminded of the book *The Breaking of the Outer Man and the Releasing of the Spirit* by Watchmen Nee. This is a powerful book concerning the releasing of the spirit of the Lord to others through brokenness. Through brokenness, I could clearly hear the voice of God.

The compassion of the Lord surrounded me daily, bottling up every one of my tears. While traveling to my hometown for the funeral I could feel God's presence cover me. Once the plane landed in Indiana, my sister Linda and her husband met me at the airport. While my brother- in- law was driving to my hometown outside of Indianapolis an overwhelming wave of grief fail over me. The tears started to flow and I begin to scream why did this happen to me, what had I done to deserve this. Hysterically crying in the back seat of the car my brother –in- law pulled over and Linda left the front and came to the back to comfort me. While my sister was praying a blanket of peace fell from heaven, the overwhelming feeling to cry and scream was gone. Immediately I stopped crying and asked Linda if she felt that, she said yes. Many believers have shared experiences about the peace of God. This peace surpasses all understanding. The peace of God is unlike any peace we have experienced on earth. The precious peace of God immediately washed away the overwhelming feeling of sorrow.

The morning of the funeral the Holy Spirit spoke to me, no weapon formed against Andrae prospered. How can this be, the weapon did not prosper, but my son was no longer with me. The Holy Spirit spoke again the weapon was formed to destroy his soul, but it did not prosper. God is so gracious and concerned with the hurt and pain of His children. The Lord healed my pain and brought me through the storm with profound revelation. Praise God for the spirit of truth, the revelation of what really happened and not what the enemy wanted my family to believe. The revelation knowledge of knowing God answered my prayers concerning the soul of my son. My constant prayer was that Andrae would never be lost, but delivered into His hands. The presence of God was in the midst of the funeral and during the altar call; many young people and family members received Christ. During the several months before the tragedy, I felt the burden to pray for young people and I made a commitment to fast and pray every Wednesday for the young people in my family, community, and my local church.

"Likewise you younger people, submit yourselves to your elders. Yes, all of you be submissive to one another, and be clothed with humility for God resists the proud, but gives grace to the humble. Therefore humble yourselves under the mighty hand of God, that He may exalt you in due time, casting all your care upon Him, for He cares for you." (I Peter 5:5-7, NKJV). In the midst of tragic

life experiences, God clothes us with humility. Even though painful situations make us weak, God becomes strong even in our weakness. In that humble place, I realized just how fragile and broken I was and how great and powerful my God is. Yes, I can honestly say this period of my life was the most humbling. Where was that strong woman who could complete several tasks at one time? Nothing, but a pile of shattered rubble fit only for the Master's use.

"The hand of the Lord came upon me and brought me out in the Spirit of the Lord, and set me down in the midst of the valley; and it was full of bones. Then He caused me to pass by them all around, and behold, there were very many in the open; and indeed they were very dry. And He said to me, "Son of man, can these bones live?" So I answered, "O Lord God, You know." Again He said to me, "Prophesy to these bones, and say to them, `O dry bones, hear the word of the Lord! Thus says the Lord God to these bones; "Surely I will cause breath to enter into you, and you shall live. I will put sinews on you and bring flesh upon you, cover you with skin and put breath in you; and you shall live. Then you shall know that I am the Lord" (Ezekiel 37:1-6 NKJV).

The outward man was completely broken into a million pieces. Just like Ezekiel answering God concerning the story of the dry bones. Can these dry bones live? Ezekiel said only you know God. Only the hand of God could pick up all the pieces and make me over again. God raised me up from that season of grief and breathed life back into me even though I was ready to let go. God breathed life back into every fiber of my being, no longer the person I use to be, but who He called me to be. Healing came through ministering to others that experienced the same pain and brokenness.

I was blessed with the wonderful opportunity to minister to women in the small town of Soroti, Uganda. After the word concerning forgiveness had gone forth, the altar call was given for people to come up for prayer. Many people came up for prayer, only God could bring them to a place of forgiveness, to forgive individuals who committed tragic acts against them and their loved ones. Every person on the team took a group of women to different areas and proceeded to minister to them. When the women begin to share their tragic stories, I realized the purpose God had on my life. We proceeded to pray for God to help us forgive and give us the ability to release the people who brought such pain and destruction to our lives. Like a fresh, rain the Holy Spirit swept through the grounds miraculously, healing, and relieving all of the heavy weight of unforgiveness. I realized the only way I could have ministered to the hurting women of Uganda was to experience the hurt firsthand.

"This is what the Lord says: Heaven is my throne, and the earth is my footstool. Where is the house you will build for me? Where will my resting place be? Has not my hand made all these things, and so they came into being, declares the Lord. This is the one I esteem: he who is humble and contrite in spirit, and trembles at my word." (Isaiah 66:1-2 NIV).

Spiritual or secular, we all have an idea of what humility means. Some people believe walking around saying I am a worm or looking sad and lowly is the biblical sense of humility. The true biblical definition of humility is a godly posture of the heart and honest obedience to God. Humility is the opposite of pride. Godly humility is realized once we recognize that God is our creator and the creator of the universe.

Making the decision to submit to the will of God and to walk in obedience is true humility. The best illustration of true humility is our Lord and savior Jesus Christ, He humbled Himself by becoming obedient to the point of death even the death of the cross. The humility of Jesus Christ brought us salvation and the very thought of Jesus dying on the cross for our sins should bring us to humility. Worship and praise opens the gate to the outer court, but true humility opens the gate to God's presence, the holy of holies. In the presence of God, there is peace, deliverance, healing, and the fullness of joy. The presence of God is life changing, chains of bondage are broken, and divine truths revealed. "The truth is this: Pride may die in you, or nothing of heaven can live in you. Under the banner of the truth, give yourself up to the meek and humble spirit of the holy Jesus. Humility must sow seed, or there can be no reaping in Heaven."[4]

Life on earth is full of swift transitions, various trials, and tribulations. Humble yourselves under the hands of the almighty God and allow Him to use every situation for His Glory. Allow God to use the crushing pain of tragedy for His glory. *"And we know that all things work together for the good to those who love God, to those who are the called according to His purpose"* (Romans 8:28 NKJV).

God will use what Satan meant for evil and work it out for our good. Everything that we go through, all that we endure in this life is all for the Glory of God. I was stripped from all that I thought I was and transformed into a true servant of God. Humility is expressed when we voluntarily submit to the will of God, humility takes self-denial. The message is to avoid pride and arrogance, realize you are inadequate in your own strength. The best definition of humility I have ever heard is this: "Humility is not denying the power you have,

but admitting that the power comes through you and not from you"[5]
For the eyes of the Lord run to and fro throughout the whole earth,
to show Himself strong on behalf of those whose heart is loyal to Him
(II Chronicles 16:9 NKJV). God is drawn to humility; His eyes roam
throughout the whole earth for those whose hearts are loyal to Him.
He is always alert and searching for yielded vessels whose heart is
blameless toward him.

"God resists (stands against, opposes, hinders) the proud
(arrogant, smug), but gives grace (help, aid, assistance, ability) the
humble"[6]

"My brethren, count it all joy when ye fall into divers' temp-
tations; knowing this, that the trying of your faith worketh patience.
But let patience have her perfect work, that ye may be perfect and
entire, wanting nothing." (James 1:2-4 KJV).

God can deliver you out of every situation. Paul said in the
book of James to count it all joy when we fall in divers' temptations,
trials, and tribulations; let patience have its perfect work in you. The
experience may be crushing, but stay in the fire and allow God to
work out the selfishness, independence, anger, unforgiveness, past
hurts, and bitterness. Allow the Holy Spirit to work through the brokenness of your life. Allow God to refine you in the fire and you shall
emerge as pure gold.

<u>Prayer for Humility</u>

Heavenly father, I worship you in the beauty of your holiness. You are my savior and my God, a very present help in trouble
times. Father your word says you resist the proud and give grace to
the humble. I declare war on the pride in my life; I declare war on

self-sufficiency and walking in my own way. My desire is to be like Jesus, humble in heart, compassionate, and sympathetic. I humble myself in brokenness, break the outer man, and release your spirit through me.

I humble myself before you now, guide me in your truth, and teach me your ways. Continue to cover me with the peace that surpasses man's understanding. Help me to stay sensitive to the voice of the Holy Spirit in Jesus name. Amen!

MINISTER BRENDA GARDNER

Minister Brenda Gardner is a powerful woman of God who walks in the love and the compassion of Christ. She presents herself as a living sacrifice unto the Lord. She is more than a conquer through the power of intercession. Through the pulling down of strongholds that hinder, people from knowing God. She is called to stand in the gap for the lost and Christians weak from the battle. Her constant walk with the Lord prepares her to minister to the broken hearted and those challenged with grief and loss.

She heard the call to ministry in 1997 and received her license in ministry in 1998. She worked in the ministry five years at New Life Anointed International Christian Center. She taught discipleship and assisted the missions department. She was blessed with the opportunity to travel overseas to Africa on several occasions. She was called to professional counseling and is presently studying Psychology at the University of Phoenix. Her passion is giving back to the community through helping the children of Henrico County in Richmond Virginia. She is an active member for CASA, an organization of volunteers giving children a voice in the juvenile court system.

CHAPTER 5

The Enjoli Woman: the Proverbs 31 Woman on Steroids

There was a TV commercial in the 1970s about Enjoli perfume. In it, a professional-looking woman danced around her home, presumably after coming home from work and sang, "I can bring home the bacon, fry it up in a pan, and never, ever let you forget you're a man…cause I'm a woman Enjoli." For me, a teenager at the time—and for many women at that time—this woman's message symbolized the birth of the superwoman. Never mind the Bionic Woman, Charlie's Angels, or Christie Love, the Enjoli woman challenged the image of all women. The Enjoli woman was the Proverbs 31 woman on steroids and I bought in to it lock, stock and barrel.

By the 1970s, not only were woman expected to be virtuous inside the home, but the role had extended to the marketplace. You may ask how the Enjoli woman fits into the postmodern society in which we live today. She has become the norm, the expectation. In fact, few of her duties in the home have changed, but her attention has turned outward. She seeks fame and fortune. She seeks to assist her family in achieving a higher standard of living, and she seeks control. As the Enjoli woman's contemporary Billie Jean King immortalized, she is a fierce competitor. She demands fair pay, equal rights, and respect. By the 1990s, these demands had become an expectation. In the year 2012, we find the discussion at the highest levels of society as the President of the United States campaigns for the Lilly Ledbetter Fair Pay Act. This is a bill the President signed into action supporting equal pay for equal work. [7]

While this seemingly radical portrait may scare off some readers and welcome others, I want to suggest that we have lost touch with what Christ has deemed important. I speak not as a repressed, underdeveloped, unsophisticated female seeking to put woman back in a subservient place. I speak rather as a well-educated, intellectual, hard working, soul-saved, washed in the blood person who happens to be female who is trying to get your attention. While the main audience I direct this chapter to herein is female, I am writing what God has inspired me to say to anyone focused on success and the trappings thereof. God is calling us back to Him. It is going to take humility to go back; it is going to take sacrifice to go back. It may even take giving up some of our creature comforts and pleasures. It is going to take focusing on God and focusing on Him alone. I believe there is a blessing in it for each of us who is willing to take the journey. I believe we will be the better for it.

"Then Jesus said to His disciples, "Assuredly, I say to you that it is hard for a rich man to enter the kingdom of heaven. And again I say to you, it is easier for a camel to go through the eye of a needle than for a rich man to enter the kingdom of God." When His disciples heard it, they were greatly astonished, saying, "Who then can be saved?" (Matthew 19:23-25 NKJV). In Matthew 19, Jesus tells us twice that it is going to be difficult for a rich man to enter

or get into the kingdom of heaven. The image of a camel trying to fit through the eye of a needle demonstrates Jesus' wonderful way of bringing the point to life. I remember threading needles for my mother when I was growing up. It was hard enough to get that thin piece of thread through the opening or eye, let alone a camel, one of the largest animals on earth.

Jesus emphasizes the point by repeating it twice in order to make it very important. Even the disciples were astonished by Jesus' hyperbole. The Bible says they were puzzled, bewildered saying, "Who then can be saved?" I am going to join the disciples on this one using the vernacular of our day and simply say 'for real?' However, Lord what about those rich folks in the Hebrew Scriptures like Jacob, Joseph, and Solomon? The Queen of Sheba was rich and she was not even part of the chosen people. What about the Scripture that says you are going to pour me out a blessing that I do not have room enough to receive? (Malachi 3:10)

I can deal with scripture. I understand scripture such as: create in me a clean heart, faith without works is dead, take up your cross daily …but You want me to be poor? Lord, do You know how long I have been striving for nice things, things I feel I deserve? Lord You know my father worked two jobs and my mother worked her fingers to the bone. They worked hard so I could go to college, get a good education, and make something out of myself. Now, You want me give it away? Matthew 6: 31 tells me not worry or be anxious over what I am going to eat or drink or wear. Lord help me to understand what You mean by my being blessed when I am poor in spirit.[8] Come on Jesus. Do You really mean that?

We are as sheep that have gone astray; we have turned every

one to his [and her or my] own way. Help us Lord to understand Your will for our lives. Thank you that Jesus has justified us by taking on and bearing the iniquity of us all. (Isaiah 53:6).

"Now it happened as they went that He entered a certain village; and a certain woman named Martha welcomed Him into her house. And she had a sister called Mary, who also sat at Jesus' feet and heard His word. But Martha was distracted with much serving, and she approached Him and said, "Lord, do You not care that my sister has left me to serve alone? Therefore tell her to help me." And Jesus answered and said to her, "Martha, Martha, you are worried and troubled about many things. But one thing is needed, and Mary has chosen that good part, which will not be taken away from her." (Luke 10:38-42 NKJV).

I have come to encourage those who are working diligently in the vineyard of home, work, and life today. I particularly want to encourage the unsung mothers and women of virtue who do so much and receive little recognition. I also seek to help each of us restore balance.

The Enjoli woman has become Martha unchecked; looking good on the outside and lauded by the world. She is trying to be a savior to many in her household, church, and community. The Enjoli woman, while potentially having a form of godliness, is really spinning out of control. Many have wondered how to slow down the merry-go-round of responsibility consisting of work, kids, spouse, aging parents, church, and beauty. King Solomon, the wisest man to live and one of the richest wrote, "vanity of vanities, all is vanity." (Ecclesiastes 1:1-2).

I can only imagine the struggle of a single parent raising kids today. If you are active and productive, you have a lot on your plate. Many of you have worked hard and long with little thanks. Not only can appreciation be virtually absent, but also one of the rewards of doing a fine job is that demands continue to increase. Being reactivated with the so-and-so committee, singing on the choir, and organizing the family reunion are just some examples.

Still other females I am talking to are single and may not have kids. They have taken on the burden and responsibility of life pretty much by themselves. Instead of crying out for others (the Marys' in her life) to come and help, she is draining herself, not only from overwork and stress, but also from one of the greatest tools of the devil, isolation. Some are blessed to be in friendship with others who help, but more are overcommitted and alone, even in a room full of people. Many are at a loss for what to do about their situation.

We have lost the sense of time for ourselves; we have lost the sense of a Sabbath. In fact, I was reviewing the 10 Commandments in a Bible Study class recently and asked the class to share which ones they felt they needed to work on. I was confounded at my turn when I searched the list and discovered I rarely take a Sabbath. Yes, I go to church regularly, but I hardly ever slow down and take a rest. Even God rested on the seventh day. I used to believe there was too much to do; too many people counting on me. All of this activity made me feel needed and I liked feeling needed. I want to congratulate all of the overachievers who are reading this for taking some timeout for self. So how do I balance the Proverbs 31 woman with the demands of today?

Several years ago, I was in the midst of taking care of my aging dad, learning a new job, working with a variety of committees at church, and singing on the choir, when the Lord spoke to me to go back to school to get another degree. I did not mind His directive; in fact, I liked the idea. However, I was stumped as to how on earth I was going to get all of it done. I could not do it on my own. I am grateful that my testimony is not that I had a nervous breakdown. It very well could have been, but God spared me and I began working through prayer and the guidance of the Lord. He made some things naturally fall away, while other things changed. Some things changed for the better and some for the worse; for instance, I was laid off my job right after purchasing a new condo.

Whoa, Lord, why me, why now? What is going on? I had to learn how to trust Him. I had to give up some things that were near and dear to me like my condo and my regular nail appointments. Thank God, He didn't cause me to have to give up my hair appointments as well. Looking back, that time was extremely stressful. However, much of what caused me major angst was so frivolous and unimportant. The strength of my testimony is *"That in all things God works for the good of those who love Him, who have been called according to His purpose."* (Romans 8:28 NIV).

We have replaced sitting at the feet of God where we are nurtured, fed spiritually, comforted and find rest, with the activities and things of this world. The devil wants to trick us into believing that taking rest, pending quality time with God, scheduling prayer and praise and Bible Study time is to be slacking. The devil will even try to convince us, especially those of us who are type A, goal-oriented, time conscious, overachievers that spending time with God is worthless and will in fact get us off schedule. Isn't that what Martha wanted Jesus to believe about Mary? Lord, Mary is slacking; please bid Mary to come here, wash the dishes, and set the table because I want every thing to be perfect for your/our dining experience. By the way, did You happen to notice our lovely chandelier in the dining room and the bathroom? Mary, please come and polish the silver before we eat.

Jesus tenderly points Martha to seeking the things of God first. That may mean that we have to drive a Honda instead of a Lexus or that we have to redirect Facebook time to be time with God in prayer and meditation. In our obedience, He seeks to pour out a blessing on us that we do not have room enough to receive. (Malachi 3:10).

Prayer

Lord God help us to humble ourselves today. Lord, help us to get off the merry-go-round and bring back balance to our lives. Not to be caught up in the Joneses, the Bejamins or the vanities of this life. You reward those that diligently seek You so help us to balance the Martha and the Mary in each of us. You were crucified, hung on a cross for our sins. We are so grateful that You love us so much. Thank you for Your mercy. Thank you for Your grace. On our best day, we are as filthy rags and You still love us. Help us to strive not for the things of man for they are temporal, but for the things of God which are eternal. Help us to reach out to you and to others when we feel so alone, or unappreciated or when we get so bogged down in life that we don't know which way is up. Teach us to enjoy lying down in green pastures and lead us beside the still, calming waters. Help the Enjoli woman to become a lover of God even more than a lover of this world. Forgive our striving Lord, give us balance. Thank you for the blessings, thank you for the wealth of the wicked that you have stored up for the righteous, but most of all we thank you for Your Son who hung on the cross so that we can live victoriously. He reigns above all. It is in Jesus precious name that we pray and say Amen

PHYLLIS CURETON

Reverend Phyllis Cureton is a native Washingtonian who has a Masters in Business Administration and close to 20 years experience in business strategy and planning. She received her call to ministry in 2003 and earned a Masters of Divinity degree from Oral Roberts University.

Reverend Cureton is an Elder at Greater Mount Calvary Holy Church in Washington, DC under the leadership of Bishop Alfred Owens and Co-Pastor Susie Owens, where she is involved in the music and substance abuse outreach ministries. Reverend Cureton serves as a Chaplain in local hospitals. She is specifically called to minister to those who are grieving and those who are struggling with mental illness.

CHAPTER 6

An Attitude of Abasement

"Unless you change and become like little children, you will never enter the Kingdom of heaven. Therefore, whoever humbles himself like this child is the greatest in the Kingdom of Heaven." (Matthew 18:3-4 NIV).

Humility means the quality of being humble, the place of total submission to God, the first calling of our journey, and the entirety of our relationship with Him...

Humility is often not taught or promoted in our world today. We, as saints exist with each other without being aware of our principle responsibility of being a humble servant. It boggles the mind how so many of us miss this all important area of our walk with Jesus, or how others don't recognized by a measure of likeness to Jesus in His own humility, but how few of us make it an important part of our walk and prayer.

I have come to the analysis that there may be many Christians who will confess their experience of humility as being similar to my own. I was a man of God that didn't know that the meekness and lowliness of my heart was an important aspect of being a disciple, just as they were of Jesus. I realized that all humility would come to those who make Jesus the object of their desire. It is to be more like Him.

Jesus was the ultimate example on humility, yet they couldn't recognize that Christ positioned Himself in a low and humble place, to show the way on how to become a servant. Often times the very commencement of our prayers and relationship with the Father should be humble and at awe of Him.

"Let us as a people study the character of Christ until our souls are filled with the love and admiration of His humility. Let us accept that, when we are broken down under a sense of our pride, and our impotence to cast it out- Jesus Christ Himself will come in and give us grace, as a part of His wondrous life within us. Let us emulate the love and humility of Jesus."[9]

"But stripped Himself [of all privileges and rightful dignity, so as to assume the guise of a servant (slave), in that He became like men and was born a human being." (Philippians: 2:7 Amplified Bible AMP).

"Whosoever shall humble himself as this little child, shall be exalted." (Matthew. 18:3 NIV). *"He that is least among you, the same shall be great."* (Luke 9:46 NIV).

What is considered as contrary to humility is pride and arrogance. Pride is known as an inflated sense of oneself, while arrogance is a by-product of pride. Arrogant people want to press their way in an overbearing manner.

"Pride goes before destruction, a haughty spirit before a fall." (Proverbs 16:18 NIV).

As a child, I recognized that my biological father was a humble man. At 5 feet 8 inches 220 lbs., his stature was considered a solid stocky man. He was able to knock a man out with one punch. Not knowing that he was my first example of what humbleness looked like. While in church, he worked as the treasurer and a deacon - servants heart for sure. I noticed that he would humble himself to leadership. He humbled himself not only to leadership, but to every person he came into contact. My father was a part-time barber for his sons and close neighbors, like Mr. Richard. Mr. Richard had seizures. We called them "having a spell." He would get violent for no apparent reason and totally forget where he was. As kids, we would run out of the house when the spells started. My dad would maintain his composure cutting his hair, while Mr. Richard would have those spells. Somehow, my father was able to calm Mr. Richard down and finish cutting his hair. My father never took the credit for the many things he did. My father is no longer with us, but he is with God in heaven. He was a great man. I surely loved my father and the life that God gave him. Now, here I am a man of God like my father, learning more and more how to be a humble servant and submissive to authority.

The following scriptures below shed light on the posture and position of humbleness that our Lord and savior showed during His time in the earth realm. *"The Son can do nothing of Himself"* (John 5:19 KJV). *"I can of My own self do nothing; My judgment is just, because I seek not Mine own will"* (John 5:30 KJV). *"I receive not glory from men"* (John 5:41 KJV). *"I am come not to do Mine own will"* (John 6:38). "My teaching is not Mine" (John 7:16 KJV). *"I am not come of Myself"* (John 7:28). *"I do nothing of Myself"* (John 8:28 KJV). *"I have not come of Myself, but He sent Me"* (John 8:42). "I seek not Mine own glory" (John 8:50) *"The words that I say, I speak not from Myself"* (John 14:10). *"The word which ye hear is not Mine"* (John 14:24). As we see, the King of Kings humbled Himself as a position of servitude for you and me to glean from.

When you read the writings of Paul in the New Testament, you began to notice that Paul's speech was becoming similar to Jesus. *"And I, brethren, when I came to you, did not come with excellence of speech or of wisdom declaring to you the testimony of God. For I determined not to know anything among you except Jesus Christ and Him crucified. I was with you in weakness, in fear, and in much trembling."* (I Corinthians 2:1-5 KJV).

"He who is humble and contrite in spirit, and trembles at my word. " (Isaiah 66:2 NIV).

Humility also means viewing others as higher than ourselves. The Greek word *"tapeinoo"* means, *"to level a mountain or a hill."* Humble people are those who have no hills rising in their hearts. They are not filled with arrogance and pride.[10]

Understanding humility is a vital part of your walk, your approach, and your relationship with the Father. I am humbled to be a servant of God who can think about Jesus and all that He has done for me. He shows me daily that he loves me. Being able to humble ourselves in the midst of adversity and strife, will catapult our wants, needs, and desires from the Lord. In result, our prayers will not be hindered when we come to Him with our petitions. I vigorously believe that the more Christ-like I am the more humble and appre hensive I will become.

Through all its existence, humility can only prevail with the life that was in the seed that gave it being. Its nature must be seen in every branch, leaf, and fruit. If humility be the first, the all-including grace of the life of Jesus, and the secret of His atonement, then the health and strength of our spiritual life will entirely depend upon Him. This makes humility the primary trait we admire in Him, and the fundamental quality we ask of Him.[11]

Begin to study the word of God as it pertains to humility. The revelation knowledge from scripture will rise from the pages of men and women showing humility at its finest. I believe one of the secrets to humility is a desire and a hunger to do God's will. You should want humility like a deer that pants after water. Go after the true meaning of humility day by day, and watch how Jesus will lead you. Learn to humble yourself, so you can be exalted.

"For whoever exalts himself will be humbled, and whoever humbles himself will be exalted." (Matthew 23:12 NIV). *"The sacrifices of God are a broken spirit: a broken spirit and a contrite heart, o God, you will not despise."* (Psalm 51:17 NIV).

"⁵Let this same attitude and purpose and [humble] mind be in you which was in Christ Jesus: [Let Him be your example in humility:] ⁸And after He had appeared in human form, He abased and humbled Himself [still further] and carried His obedience to the extreme of death, even the death of the cross! ⁹Therefore [because He stooped so low] God has highly exalted Him and has [ᶠ]freely bestowed on Him the name that is above every name..." (Philippians: 2:5, 8, 9 AMP).

"The exceeding greatness of God's power is waiting to be re

vealed through those who are humble enough and small enough for God to use! Constant service with gracious humility, constant helpfulness with a sense of total submission, constant awareness of God's greatness and personal nothingness is the measure of a soul truly ample in the sight of the Lord."

Lord Jesus, I must begin my day by confessing that my heart has often been deceived into thinking that I am living a life of humble service when in reality, many of my motivations are grounded in selfishness. Father today I pray that You would create in me a clean heart and renew a right spirit within me. As I clothe myself in humility, teach me Your ways. I pray that others may be esteemed and preferred more than I. Lord, grant me the grace to desire it. Free me from the desire to be exalted in any way except by You. Give me distaste for selfishness and pride. Protect me as I decrease so that You may increase. Cause my heart to flutter at Your presence. Allow me to fall on my face as dead, so You may raise me up. Father You said that You resist the proud, but give grace to the humble. Father, I humble myself before you, so that You can use me as the servant You've called me to be. Take my heart and my mind and promote the Kingdom through me. Give me a word of knowledge made to encourage and cause humility to become an immediate response from your people. Help us to change from pride and arrogance as we draw closer to You. Help me to never do anything that could bring harm to others by stepping out in anything other than the authority of the Holy Spirit. Father, you keep me humble in heart, grant me the nature of a true servant, and give me discernment and wisdom to be able to take my stand against the enemy and his evil attempts to counterfeit and destroy that which You have been preparing for me. Lord let the words of my mouth and the meditation of my heart is acceptable in Your sight, because You are my strength and my redeemer. In Jesus mighty name I pray, Amen.

MINISTER TERRY HESTER

If there is one central theme, in which I have always believed, it is this: the secret of life is to have a personal relationship with Jesus. At the age of 17, I joined the United States Marine Corps. I quickly learned what it takes to be a man first, then a warrior. My mother and father had taught me how to pray and told me that God will protect me wherever I go. The military life drew me away from my relationship with Christ. I fell deeper and deeper into sin and the cares of the world, which caused my heart to harden. I had no respect for life and all things Godly. In 1983 I married, my wife began a life as a husband and became the father of five beautiful girls. Prior to retiring from military service, I spoke to my mom. Before hanging up the phone, my mom said; "Terry, once you get out, you're going to need the Lord in your life." She was right. In the winter of 1996, 6 months after retirement, I was saved! Without the Lord in your life, there's no telling where I would be. Saints humble yourself before the mighty hand of God, and He will always lift you up. Amen.

Minister Terry Hester is a member of Strong Tower Ministries in Fredericksburg, VA where Apostle Kevin Mihlfield is Senior Pastor. Terry currently serves as the Director of Altar Response Ministry.

CHAPTER 7

Submit Yourselves

I often thought about what God meant when He said David was a man after His heart who would do all of His will. Pondering this question, I decided to study David. During the time I studied David, I found that he made many mistakes, just as we all do. Yet every time he did wrong, he made it right with God in the end. After noticing this, I soon realized that God was referring to David's humility and obedience to His voice. Whenever David was in trouble, he knew that the only one he could go to was God. I learned that in the same way, we should always go to God for repentance and guidance. We find many lessons and examples that teach us how to humble others and ourselves before God through David's stories throughout the bible.

One example can be found in Psalm 51, when Nathan, the Prophet, went to David after David had been intimate with another man's wife, Bathsheba. After hearing God's word through Nathan, David humbled himself by asking God for forgiveness. He didn't try to argue with God because he knew that what he did was wrong. Another example of when David humbled himself before God was in first Samuel. Saul was going to kill David out of jealousy because-God made David King of Israel in place of Saul. In the story, David had two chances to kill Saul. He was so close one time that he even cut off a corner of Saul's robe. However, after that incident, David said, *"The Lord forbid that I should do this thing to my Master the Lords anointed, to stretch out my hand against him, seeing he is the anointed of the Lord"* (I Samuel 24:6 NKJV). In this way, David let God handle his enemies, instead of taking actions into his own hands. Even with all the turmoil, David was doing all he could to keep the peace with Saul. And if that wasn't enough, when Saul and his sons were killed, David and his men mourned, fasted, and wept for him. Now this is what I call humility.

The word of God says *"And whoever exalts himself will be humbled and whoever humbles himself will be exalted"* (Matthew 23:12 NIV). A humble heart always thinks of others before themselves. As Jesus did for us when He came to this earth and died for us over 2000 years ago, we need to have the same selflessness. Jesus went to the Mount of Olives to pray as He often did and this was His prayer to God *"Father if it is Your will, take this cup away from Me; nevertheless not My will, but Yours, be done"* (Luke 22:42 NKJV). Jesus never prayed selfish prayers. I couldn't say that I would have prayed a selfless prayer in my beginning Christian years. But, as we continue to do less of what we want to do and take on the things of Jesus, we can have the mind of Christ and begin to think as He would think. Sometimes it's hard to do the right thing, but if it means helping someone else to be in a better place, then we, as Christians, should do it! Jesus died for us so that we would have time to get our life together and be reconciled with our Heavenly Father. And if Jesus died on the cross for us, we should do things for others with no hesitation. We often can't look to many people we know for advice on being humble because no one is perfect. But, there was and still is someone who exemplified humility perfectly, and it was Jesus Christ. Jesus was the ultimate example of a meek man with a gentle spirit. He came on this earth to show us how to live and be humble before God; He even clothed himself with humility. He did not come to be served, but to serve and He never blessed anyone with any intentions other than to show them love and the way to enter into the kingdom of God.

We shouldn't think of ourselves more highly then we ought to, for pride comes before a fall nor should we do anything for selfish gain. One of Jesus' greatest commandments is to love one another as He loved us, and encourage our neighbors. We should never use excuses, saying, "I don't feel like it" There were times when Jesus was tired, but the Bible says He still healed, He still delivered, and He still set people free. When the 5000 followers were hungry for food, He didn't just continue on the route He was travelling on, ignoring all of them. He stopped and took the time to feed them and then taught them about the word of God; as always, Jesus never put Himself first, but He remembered His purpose - to do the will of the Father.

When his disciples asked Him how to pray He gave them an example of what a prayer should be. He even prayed for them and He prays for us today because He is our advocate. He's always thinking about us. He considers, our needs, the things we go through while we are on this earth. So why is it so hard for us to return the favor? We need to humble ourselves and think of Him first. Isn't that what He is doing for us every day just by waking us up every morning? I thank God we still have examples through the written word that show us we can always open up and He will show us the way to handle every situation. He had us on His mind and was thinking of our past, present and future. If we want to follow Him, we must do as He says, "Then he said to the crowd, *"If any of you want to be my followers, you must turn from your selfish ways, take up your cross daily, and follow me."* (Luke 9:23 NLT).

I was born in a family of nine girls and one boy. There were 12 of us altogether, including my parents in the house at one time and we were always told to share whatever we had: clothes, toys, candy etc. Because we were living among so many people, we had to learn to do things for the people around us. We always made food for our family and friends. If someone was sick, had a child, or had passed away, our family was always standing together and attempting to help in any way possible. As an adult, I still have that same spirit in me. No matter how God chooses to bless me, I will always bless others with my time or in any way, I can help them. Now that I am a parent, I share with my family, the same values instilled in me as a child. I encourage this same act of kindness to be mutually shared amongst all of us. So if your neighbor needs help? Be the first to help them. If they need encouragement, let them know how much Jesus loves them. Real humility listens. Sometimes our neighbors, friends, and family go through a lot in life and they don't always know how to handle their grief or pain from life's circumstances. As

Christians, we need to listen. We need to be attentive to what they are saying, and we shouldn't judge them. Jesus never judged us even when we are wrong.

In order for us to lead people to Christ, we must first show ourselves friendly and be a good witness to what God has done in our lives. We are the body of Christ and we must work together to keep the body healthy. We must be open to what God is doing and how He wants to use us and because of this, our humility is key. Remember it's not about you. It's all about the kingdom and winning souls to Christ.

When my Husband was in the Military, we were stationed in Yuma, Arizona. My next-door neighbor was an older woman named Mrs. Battle, who at the time was about 75 years old. She belonged to a church and invited me to fellowship with her church family many times. When I first came to Arizona, I was not going to a church. I actually had not been a part of a church since I had joined the military; due to this, my heart had grown hard. I loved God, but I was not reading my bible. Mrs. Battle would come and ask me if I wanted to go to church with her and I would always make up excuses on why I couldn't go. She wouldn't push me, but she would give me gentle nudges such as, "Maybe next week." or "They are having a special speaker at the church." Each day I spoke to her, my heart began to soften because she was so nice and full of love. She would bring me homemade apple pie or lemons from her tree in her back yard, or homemade peanut brittle that was so delicious. One day she asked me again if I wanted to go to church and I said, "I have 3 kids and church does not have a daycare." She said, "I will help you." I reluc tantly said yes, thinking that if I said yes, she wouldn't have to keep asking me. When I went with Mrs. Battle to church on that Sunday, all I could do was cry. I was finally in church; I felt the presence of the Lord, and so much love from the people at the church. What really changed my heart was the love that Mrs. Battle showed me. Even though I turned her down many times before saying yes, she never made me feel guilty or forced herself on me. She always checked on me, would always bring me recipes, and she genuinely cared for me. She showed me the love of Christ through how she treated me, until Jesus prepared my heart to say yes, I will go. She has since passed away however; I will always remember the Godly love she showed me. She loved me back to where I needed to be, at the feet of Jesus. The kind of love and kindness that Mrs. Battle showed me is what we all need. It is an unconditional love. It requires a humble spirit to think of others needs before your own. She could have just gone to church every Sunday and not ask me, but she wasn't selfish at all. She gave me what God gave her, which was love and patience. We must continue to follow the life of Jesus. I know she has received her crown. Now is the time to open up and begin to look at where we are and where Jesus wants us to be. We should say that we want to be humble before Jesus and before our neighbors. We want to meet them where they are so we may win souls to Christ. I want my life to be an example for others to follow just like Mrs. Battle, because she loved Jesus. I thank God for all the humble people that He has put in my life. I have truly learned a lot from them including my mother and father.

I am forever changed by the selfless acts that they have shown me.

"Since God chose you to be the holy people he loves, you must clothe yourselves with tenderhearted mercy, kindness, humility, gentleness, and patience. Make allowance for each other's faults, and forgive anyone who offends you. Remember, the Lord forgave you, so you must forgive others. Above all, clothe yourselves with love, which binds us all together in perfect harmony." (Colossians 3:12-14 New Living Translation NLT).

<u>Prayer</u>

Father, I am forever captured by the love You have for us. For Your tender mercies are new every morning. You gave so much of yourself while you were here, and yet You continue to do so. I stand in awe of You. My life is now Yours. Father, will you please fill the void in the hearts of every believer with Your presence, and flood our hearts with Your love. Make hearts of stone hearts of flesh so You can mold and reshape them. Break our hearts for the things that break Your heart that we may obtain what You have for us - unconditional love. May we begin to walk in humility, putting the needs of others before our own. And for every non-believer, Lord, draw them close to You by Your loving kindness that they may be changed, delivered, and made free. Renew, revive, and refresh their hearts. Do it for them, Father God, just as You did it for me, In Jesus name, Amen.

MINISTER ANGELINE D. HESTER

Minister Angeline D. Hester was born in Cleveland, Ohio to Mark Jr. & Lillie Mae Wynn who has since gone to be with the Lord. She is from a family of 10, eight sisters, and one brother. Angeline confessed Jesus Christ as her Lord and Savior at the age of nine. After graduating from high school, she went into the Marine Corps where she served 4 years. While serving in the military, she met her husband of 28 years Terry Hester. Angeline and Terry are the proud parents of five beautiful girls, and four grandchildren.

Angeline is a member of Strong Tower Ministries located in Fredericksburg, VA where Apostle Kevin Mihlfeld is Senior Pastor. She currently serves with her husband Minister Terry L. Hester on the Altar Response Ministry. She has also traveled to Israel, ministered the word, and helped with missions work in Uganda, Africa.

Angeline is a loving wife; mother, grandmother, and woman of God who loves to encourage others. Her walk with the Lord has truly been life changing. Angeline is a worshipper who loves to sit at the feet of Jesus and it shows in the life that she lives for God. She's a woman after Gods own heart. Angeline ministers in the areas of prayer, praise and worship, choir, and women's ministry and was called years ago to be one of God's Intercessors on the earth today for such a time as this.

VOLUME TWO - SEEK

TABLE OF CONTENTS

VOLUME II SEEK

CHAPTER 1

Seeking Him in the Dark

Darkness has been an active force in the earth since the beginning of time (Genesis 1:2). Darkness has threatened to create an intense fear upon God's creation (Genesis 15:12). Darkness has a purpose of blinding the eyes and hiding the truth of God (I John 2:11 I Corinthians 4:5). Darkness skillfully obscures our direction and darkens our paths (John 12:25). Darkness is described as something arising from or showing evil traits or desires; something being deprived of light [i.e. knowledge, understanding, truth, or goodness].

Many circumstances that we have encountered in our lives, sickness, divorce, death of a loved one, and disappointments have ignited darkness to operate against us. When these trials and tribulations come (I Peter 4:12) the enemy is seeking for a way to position darkness around us for our demise and complete destruction. Since the God of our Lord and Savior Jesus Christ is fully aware of these coming trials and tribulations, He has purposefully made a way of escape from the works of darkness (I Corinthians 10:13). Every moment of our existence is laid out before the Lord of Host (Hebrews 4:13). It has been declared that we are more than conquerors in Christ Jesus.

But, how do we stand in this victorious position when darkness threatens our path? The Father is seeking to find us in a trium phant position in our darkest hour. He desires to find us praying as His Son did before He was crucified (Mark 14:32-42). In every way, the Father desires for us to be in the image and likeness of His Son, our Savior Jesus Christ. He desires for us to proclaim "not what I will, but what you will." He doesn't want this to be mere repeated words, but a bleeding desire from our hearts. You see the Father is not expecting us not to feel anything while we are going through our darkest hour. In Chapter 14 of Mark, Jesus went through a range of emotions in His darkest hour. He felt distressed, troubled, overwhelmed, and weak. He even asked that He not go through what He was about to face, the cruelest death known to man, a crucifixion. But, somewhere in the midst of these emotions, He found faith and love for His Father. He understood that the Father could rescue Him from the impending darkness because He said, "everything is possible for you." There also was such a deep love displayed in Jesus' prayer to the Father simply by what He called Him "Abba Father." the love that He had for His Father helped to finalize His prayer by saying "not what I will, but what you will." We must ask ourselves; in our darkest hour can we sincerely give up our will for His will?

Exchanging our will for His will is only one essential ingredient to finding Him in our darkest hour. As we yield ourselves to prayer, Jesus does not want us only focusing on the circumstance that is distressing and troubling us. He wants us to incorporate more essential ingredients in our prayer time. He desires for us to proclaim who He is, also known as worship, and invite His Holy Spirit to help us with the situation. You see, darkness threatens to make us apathetic towards prayer and immobilizes our efforts. Darkness wants us to believe that God knows all about our troubles therefore, we don't need to pray. But, God's word proclaims that we must pray without ceasing (I Thessalonians 5:17). It proclaims that we must make our request known to God.

If we make a conscious decision not to pray about a matter, we have made the conscious decision to sabotage our deliverance from darkness. Praying is not a ritual of begging for God's help or expounding on the problem, it is yielding ourselves to pray the will of God in the earth by the Holy Spirit. It is the Holy Spirit that knows how we ought to pray and it is this very reason why asking for the help of the Holy Spirit is another critical element of prayer. The Holy Spirit was sent to us, God's people, to help us in every area of our lives (John 16:7). The Holy Spirit will reveal the truths of God when we are confused because He is the Spirit of Truth. When the Holy Spirit speaks to us, He will not say anything that He hasn't heard the Father and our Savior say (John 16:13). He will reveal the heart of God! I encourage you to intentionally ask the Holy Spirit to help you in the trials you face, for He is committed to helping you through your darkest hour to the glory of Jesus Christ.

Just as the Holy Spirit is committed to glorifying Jesus Christ, we too should be committed to bringing glory to God even in our darkest hour. During our hardest times, it is important to ask the Holy Spirit to teach us how to worship Jesus Christ. Worship is an essential element in our walk with Jesus Christ. Jesus is seeking those who are worshipping Him in spirit and in truth (John 4:23). We cannot omit worship from our prayer life. Worship causes our spirit to connect with the Holy Spirit. Worship causes our heart to break for what the Father wants. Worship transforms our heart. Worship leads us into praying the will of God and not praying amiss.

Worship focuses our hearts and minds on Jesus Christ. Worship elevates Jesus above everything. Worship causes us to hear the Holy Spirit more clearly. Worship causes us to fall deeper in love with Jesus. I repeat we cannot omit worship from our prayer time! I even challenge you, beloved reader, to have a "worship only" time with God. This time will only be to worship Jesus the Christ. This time is not to ask for anything or to make Him aware of a situation. It is to solely proclaim who He is. If you know Him as a provider, then tell Him "Jesus you are my awesome provider." If you have received a revelation that He is the King of Glory, then proclaim to Him "Wonderful Jesus, you are the King of Glory, forever and ever." Worship is simply telling Him who He is.

If we, the believers of Jesus Christ, incorporate the ingredients of sincerely proclaiming, "not what I will, but what you will, deliberately." And consciously invite the Holy Spirit to help us with the trials and tribulations we face, worship Jesus Christ, unhindered and from our spirit. We will experience a greater presence of Jesus Christ, the Holy Son of God in our lives. We would undoubtedly experience a greater weight of His Holy Spirit. Even in our darkest hour, our Father, Jesus Christ and the Holy Spirit desires us to experience the fullness God and this can definitely be achieved through having a prayer life that is consistent and full of worship.

A Prayer for the Reader

Precious and Loving Father, I glorify you in all of your splendor and holiness. I exalt you Christ Jesus in all of Your wonders and might. To you be the glory and honor forever and ever. Christ Jesus, You are exalted above the heavens and the earth.

You are above everything that is grand in the world's sight. You are the King of Glory forever and ever. You are the Lord God strong and mighty. You dear Jesus, are our strong tower. You are the lifter of our heads and the giver of our daily strength. You are exalted forever Jesus, our King and redeemer. Holy is thy name forever and ever. Holy Spirit, thank you for the work that you do to glorify Jesus, The Risen Savior. Thank you for knowing the mind of Christ and revealing it to His people. Thank you King Jesus for sending your Spirit to help and comfort the people of God. Lord God Almighty, I thank you for the eyes that are reading this book and the hearts that are receiving what you have led every author to write. We bless you King Jesus for how these teachings, wisdoms, and revelations are being engraved in the hearts of your people for Your glory. We bless you sovereign and wise God for how you have made a way of escape for my brother/sister in their darkest hour. We thank you that it is Your will for us to be free from bondage. I pray in the name of Jesus Christ that the Holy Spirit will work to break every chain, fetter, and bondage from the life of my brother/sister. Holy Spirit we invite you to show us the light of God in our darkest hour. Holy Spirit teach us how to exchange our will for Jesus' will and as we receive this divine direction, we glorify You, Jesus our King, and deliverer. Awesome Jesus, thank you for the power and authority that you have given my sister/brother through Your death on the cross. I pray dear Jesus that you would keep my brother/sister's feet from falling. I pray that Your blood would be upon them, protecting them from the wiles of the enemy. I pray that my brother/sister will be fully covered with the armor of God and the blood of Jesus Christ. Lord Jesus cover their households with your precious blood.

Cover their children with your precious blood. Cover their marriages with your precious blood. Cover their minds, body, and spirits with your precious blood. Keep them safe of any incidents or accidents and be their rear guard as they continue to press toward the mark in you Christ Jesus. We bless you Christ Jesus for a fervent and consistent prayer life for my brother/sister. A prayer life that yearns to be in constant fellowship with you and the Holy Spirit; and a prayer life that longs to hear the voice of the Lord and hungers after the word of God. You Christ Jesus is worthy of all the praise, glory and honor. I believe you are doing a wonderful work in the heart of my brother/sister right now and I glorify you for this work. Thank you Lord Jesus for your love towards us, in Jesus Name, Amen.

PROPHETESS MASADA FARA JOHNSON

Prophetess Masada Fara Johnson is a native Washingtonian born to devote Muslim parents, Geraldine El-Ameen and Hamza Hameed.

In 1991, Masada heard an audible voice say, "go to the big church on the corner." Immediately she knew she had to go to Free Gospel Deliverance Temple, where the Honorable Bishop Ralph E. Green presides. Over the next 7 years, the "big church on the corner" was essential in laying a firm Christ centered deliverance foundation.

Over the years, she had the privilege of serving and receiving prophetic impartation through the teaching and prophetic ministry of Bishop Thomas W. Weeks, Jr. In 2005, the Lord led Masada under the pastoralship of Bishop Don Meares and under the leadership of Elder/Prophet Peyton Gray of Evangel Cathedral where she was entrusted to lead a thriving Intercessory Prayer ministry and currently serves as an ordained deacon. Within this season, the Lord allowed Masada's path to intersect with Apostle Tonya Smallwood, founder of Sisters of the SON Ministries.

Masada was also blessed to be under the leadership, mentorship and spiritual tutelage of Apostle Tonya for several years as the Lord continued to use these incredible leaders to develop a powerful intercessor and prophet.

Masada has been an administrative professional for over 20 years working for attorneys, Vice Presidents, Sr. Vice Presidents and a CEO. She is the founder of Vision Fulfilled, Inc., a not-for profit organization focusing on helping the less fortunate by feeding the homeless, organizing food and clothing drives for shelters and low income families, and creating and facilitating life skill workshops for women, men and teens.

Masada had served as an intercessor for PrayLive, an internet radio broadcast, reaching thousands of souls across many nations. Masada's heart is not only fervent for intercession and the prophetic, but for also being a soul winner in the streets of Washington DC and surrounding areas. Masada is an effective leader in exhorting saints to their rightful position in the body of Christ and training groups and individuals on how to effectively win souls to Christ through the leading of the Holy Spirit.

Masada lives in Maryland and has been blessed with two precious daughters, Daija and Levonna.

CHAPTER 2

Be Transparent in Prayer

Have you ever notice that at most churches the regularly scheduled prayer service is the least attended service? Even choir rehearsals are generally higher in attendance than prayer meetings. However when there is a problem people rush to the sanctity of prayer. I haven't quite grasped why people struggle with prayer. So many times people shy away from prayer because they say they don't know how to pray or during prayer, they run out of words to say. Prayer is a form of communication with God. It's also a time of casting every care and concern on Him and asking Him for guidance. We don't have to put on airs or pretenses when we go to God in prayer. *"For we have not an high priest which cannot be touched with the feeling of our infirmities; but was in all points tempted like as we are, yet without sin. Let us therefore come boldly unto the throne of grace, that we may obtain mercy, and find grace to help in time of need."* (Hebrews 4:15-16 KJV).

Recently I was watching a documentary about Facebook and how it has crippled our generation in so many ways. While Facebook is beneficial as a place of connecting to family and friends all over the world, it has distorted our perception of reality and virtual persona.

Social networking sites like Facebook, MySpace, Twitter and the like allow us to fill out online forms or profiles to describe ourselves. We access these sites from the comfort of our homes, where we enter information about our likes, dislikes, beliefs, ages and backgrounds. We then attach an attractive picture to the profile and there you have it! Instantly the world sees you in all of your perfection and glory.

However, a form that you filled out in the comfort of our homes doesn't always give the world an honest view of the person in the home. While you are posing perfectly on your profile picture with all of your accomplishments listed on your page the reader doesn't know that the bill for the credit card you purchased that camera with take the picture is 90 days past due. Neither does your on-line "friend" know that the house you are posing in is in foreclosure. Although your status is married and the pictures of you and your spouse are posted on your wall, the reader doesn't know that you are on the verge of divorce. Social networking has allowed us to become great pretenders for the sake of image and acceptance.

Although we feel the pressure to be perfect in the virtual world, thankfully we don't have to pretend with God. He knows the number of hairs on your head. He also knows the intent of your heart. Therefore, be confident that your Creator knows you inside and out and there is nothing about you that surprises Him. God had you in His plan before the foundation of the world. *"Before I formed thee in the belly I knew thee; and before thou camest forth out of the womb I sanctified thee, and I ordained thee a prophet unto the nations."*

(Jeremiah1:5 KJV). God was not only giving Jeremiah this assurance, but also letting mankind know that He knew our attributes, characterist ics, and abilities even before the foundation of the world. God had us on His mind before Mark Zuckerberg created Facebook! We are not validated because of clever Facebook statuses or picture perfect profiles. We are validated because we were chosen by God to be conformed in the image of Jesus Christ. *"For whom he did foreknow, he also did predestinate to be conformed to the image of his Son, that he might be the firstborn among many brethren."* (Romans 8:29 KJV). Since we know, there is nothing about us that surprises God we should enter into prayer with a transparent spirit. It may not be easy to be transparent with people, but you can always be transparent with God. My mother and my grandmother taught me that I could talk to them about anything. No subject has ever been off limits. I was always encouraged and instructed to tell the truth to my mother even if I had done something wrong. I've developed a mindset in my adult life that it's better for me to tell the ugly truth as opposed to a pretty lie. This mindset extends far beyond communicating with my mother, grandmother and people in general. I've also developed this mindset in my relationship with God and in my prayer life.

I believe this mentality really developed when I was experiencing a failing marriage. I was hurt and frustrated. I would pray for things to get better in my marriage and it seemed to get worse. I was faithful in church and I still saw no improvement at home. My burdened heart became frustrated and all of the deep and spiritual words I was using in prayer dried up. I was hurting and I didn't have much more to say to God except, "Lord this hurts!" I started talking to God the way I would talk to a girlfriend. I began to just pour my heart out to God in broken English, bad grammar, and raw emotions. Venting my real feelings to God seemed to bring me closer to Him.

I didn't feel like I was a minister presenting a situation to my pastor in the best form or fashion. I truly began to feel like a daughter crying out to her Father for help. My natural father died when I was nine years old so I really began to cling to my Heavenly Father like daddy's little girl. That's when I started hearing from Him more clearly. That's when I started feeling the comfort from my Heavenly Father.

Prayer became my place of comfort. Prayer time truly became my "secret place" where I could get away from the dysfunction of my abusive marriage. It was in prayer and worship that I escaped my present distress and saw a brighter future. I discovered that I didn't have to pretend in prayer. As a minister, I was ashamed that my family was falling apart and I tried to hide my pain. But, when I went to God in prayer, I could reveal my true feelings. I told God that I didn't want to be in this painful marriage any longer but I was also afraid to leave. I asked God for signs and clarity about how to proceed. I didn't have the answers and I didn't trust the opinions of my family. I already knew they wanted me to leave because they were tired of seeing me hurt. Even with the dysfunction, the abuse and the dishonor in the marriage I wanted God to fix the marriage more than I wanted to walk away. But, it was in God's will for me to leave. It took shutting out the opinions of loved ones and seeking God in prayer to know without a shadow of a doubt that it was time to go.

Leaving wasn't easy, but God made a way of escape and provided me the opportunity and means to leave when it was time. Although I was afraid to start over and live a new life as a single parent, I knew that I could go to God in prayer about every emotion I was feeling at any given time. I experienced every emotion imaginable as I transitioned from being married with a child, a home, and sharing living expenses to a single mother renting an apartment and paying all of the expenses alone. There were times I was angry with my husband for not trying harder to keep our family together. There were days I was mad at myself for leaving although I know without a shadow of a doubt it was time. There were days I felt guilty and blamed myself for not trying hard enough. There were even days I was mad at God for not fixing the problems for us! There were many days and nights I cried. There were nights I cried myself to sleep. Thankfully, my Creator understood my pain and didn't punish me when I threw my temper tantrums. After I would vent and question God, He would always comfort me through His word. He reminded me that He would never leave me nor forsake me. God's word can be a soothing balm to any wound. Even through the tears and heartache, I knew that God was with me.

I want to encourage you to be honest and transparent about how you feel when you go to God in prayer. Prayer is communication between you and God. Talk to God just like you would talk to a friend. He already knows what you are faced with and He's able to deliver you out of your troubles. *"And it shall come to pass, that before they call, I will answer; and while they are yet speaking, I will hear."* (Isaiah 65:24 KJV). God is in anticipation of hearing from you! Don't ever be ashamed to pray. Even if you have sinned, God wants to hear repentance from you. If you are coming to God with joy in your heart and with praise, He still wants to hear from you. Just like your best friend enjoys sitting down with you laughing and enjoying great conversation, it is the same with God.

He loves to spend time with you communing and sharing. As you pray, talk to God, then be quiet and let Him talk to you. Train your spiritual ear to hear the voice of God. Know that God is never going to speak contrary to His word. So, I encourage you to keep your bible close during prayer. It is also important to keep a pen and notebook close to you while in prayer because as He speaks. You want to be able to capture what the Spirit is saying to you in that moment.

No matter what you are faced with, don't be ashamed to take it to God in prayer. We don't have to pretend with Him. He doesn't expect us to have picture perfect "timelines" and spiritual "profiles" all the time like we see on Facebook. Be honest and truthful with the Lord because He already knows. When you are hurting don't be ashamed to tell Him. When you are sad, express that to God. When you are lonely, you don't have to pretend you don't need companionship. When you are angry, tell God what is making you feel that way. When you have sinned, please go to God and ask for forgiveness. You can be real with God! He is still in the forgiving business. He's also ready to restore you. *"Seek ye the LORD while he may be found, call ye upon him while he is near: Let the wicked forsake his way, and the unrighteous man his thoughts: and let him return unto the LORD, and he will have mercy upon him; and to our God, for he will abundantly pardon."* (Isaiah 55:5-7 KJV).

Prayer

Heavenly Father, I come to you on behalf of my brothers and sisters reading this book. I pray that you would comfort them right where they are and in what they are going through. You are their Creator and You know everything about them. There is no issue that will ever catch you off guard. God I pray that you would help them to know that they can come to You as their problem solver. I pray for their spiritual ears to be in tuned with your word and your voice. Let them hear from you with clarity. I pray for a fresh desire for prayer. Let them desire to seek you early in the morning so that you can give them instructions to guide them through the day. In the name of Jesus, I rebuke the spirit of guilt and shame that would hinder them from approaching your throne with confidence; knowing you will forgive and have mercy on them when needed. Lord I pray that this prayer serves as agreement between every reader and myself that we are touching and agreeing concerning their prayer request. I pray that you would instill a new hunger and thirst for your righteousness in my brothers and sisters reading this book. Father as they seek you, let them be comforted in the revelation you will grant them in your will and in your word. We believe now that it is already done. We thank you for supernatural manifestation. We claim it to be so. In Jesus Name. Amen.

DISTRICT ELDER KECIA SIMS

District Elder Kecia Sims is known as a powerful preacher, a teacher with a sense of humor and a counselor with a compassionate ear. The ministry of District Elder Sims has been experienced in many denominations and churches throughout the country. She currently serves as Pastor of Prophetic Worship Center, Inc. AAF in San Leandro, CA. She serves as District Elder of the Western District of the Apostolic Assemblies Fellowship, Inc.

She is the published author of "Loving The Addict, Hating The Addiction." This book serves to encourage Christian families coping with the struggle of drug addiction. She has also published "Reflections" prayer journal that encourages women to write down their precious thoughts and victorious praises as God speaks to them.

Filled with many gifts and talents, she has labored in the vineyard in many different capacities. She is a dedicated mother. She is a California Certified Domestic Violence Counselor. She has appeared on many radio shows and hosted her very own live television talk show, Destiny with Kecia Sims.

District Elder Kecia is a very ambitious woman who is not afraid to take a "risk" for Jesus! She understands that the trials she had to experience over the years was for a testimony to minister to others For the Furtherance of the Gospel.

CHAPTER 3

Come A Little Closer

"Hear, O LORD, when I cry with my voice: have mercy also upon me, and answer me. When thou saidst, Seek ye my face; my heart said unto thee, Thy face, Lord, will I seek." (Psalm 27:7-8 KJV).

In these present times, many seek numerous ways to satisfy the need to succeed in life. The search for success and self-gratification often leads to the violation of God's laws and principles. This can be seen through destructive activities such as stealing, cheating, alcohol and drug abuse, premarital sex and much more. Even in the minds of some in the Body of Christ, the way to successfully seek and fulfill God's plans and purposes is confined to involvement in various church committees, programs, and ministry groups. In many cases, the participation in prayer and intercessory groups is minimal. Communicating with God through prayer, corporately or individually, has taken a back seat to the more visible ministries. This journey for success may lead down some pathways, back roads, and encounters that are contrary to God's will. *"There is a way which seemeth right unto a man, but the end thereof is the ways of death."* (Proverbs 14:12 KJV).

The Dictionary definition for seek[13] is to search for is for, to try; attempt. Some of the synonyms for seek[14] as defined in Thesaurus.com are: be after, beat the bushes, chase, look high and low, leave no stone unturned, track down and pursue.

In the Bible, words for "seek" mean to seek the face of God; to desire; to examine or explore; to seek earnestly; to diligently search; to wish for; to crave; to investigate; to pursue. Jeremiah 24:7 reads, "I will give you a heart to know me." Our loving Father desires that we become intimate with Him and has given us a heart to do so. However, closeness with God and being in His presence comes as we desire and take action to know His will and ways and to experience His love. *"And without faith it is impossible to please God, because anyone who comes to him must believe that he exists and that he rewards those who earnestly seek him."* (Hebrews 11:6 NIV). Faith works through love.

For I know the thoughts that I think toward you, saith the LORD, thoughts of peace, and not of evil, to give you an expected end. Then shall ye call upon me, and ye shall go and pray unto me, and I will hearken unto you. And ye shall seek me, and find me, when ye shall search for me with all your heart." (Jeremiah 29:11-13 KJV).

Seeking God through prayer is one of the ways and key ingredient to become closer to Him. An effective prayer life is one of the most important elements in the believer's Christian walk and must be based on the word of God. Prayer along with spending time with God through studying the word is about desire and love for Him. It is not just a dutiful routine or discipline in the Christian walk. God desires our prayer lives to be easy flowing and enjoyable.

He wants our prayers to be truthful and heartfelt, not entangled with legalism and obligation. Now, we know that the Satan comes to deter us from any intimate time with the Lord in many ways.

"The thief cometh not, but for to steal, and to kill, and to destroy: I am come that they might have life, and that they might have it more abundantly." (John 10:10 KJV). Resist the devil. Change your focus. Meditate on the word of God and believe what the word says. Declare and decree His promises out of your mouth. Began to worship your Lord for who He is and praise Him for what He has done. Jesus came so we can live full and rich lives in Him. The devil has to flee!

As I have grown spiritually, I recognize more and more the need to and benefits of seeking the face of God through prayer for all areas of my life and the lives of others. Looking back over my life's experiences, I can see how much He loves us and what lengths He will go to reach us. I can recount the times and stages of how God has drawn me closer to Him by His Spirit. I can also recount the times when I resisted the drawing of the Spirit. Most of my actions were a result of lack of knowledge and understanding of the word and the move of the Holy Spirit. Other actions were just violating the word of God I did know. I will share with you a little of my life story in hopes that it will encourage you to seek His face and develop a closer relationship with Him through prayer.

"Train up a child in the way he should go: and when he is old, he will not depart from it." (Proverbs 22:6 KJV). I grew up in Norfolk, Virginia. My families were members of a Baptist church and my parents made sure I attended. I joined church at a young age was an active participant in many church based activities including

Sunday school classes, Easter and Christmas plays. Memorizing and reciting scriptures was a must and a part of my weekly routine.

When I was very young, my grandmother who I called Mama lived with us for a period of time. My dad and aunt would refer to her as prophet because she would know what they had been up to before they told her. I remember her as a woman who had a beautiful singing voice. I was told she was a member of the Church of God in Christ where she would be the featured singer on the local radio program. While Mama was cooking and cleaning, I would hear her singing songs like "Precious Lord Take My Hand" and " The Lord's Prayer "As she would sing, I began to learn the songs and sing with her. I mostly remember Mama as always reading the bible and a woman of fervent prayer. We slept on a portable cot in the living room of our one bedroom home. Each night, we would kneel beside the bed together and she would pray for me. Then, I would repeat the Lord's Prayer after her. In my young mind, questions began to rise in me as to "Who is this God that my grandmother sings about and prays to all of the time? How did she get such a close relationship with Him? She seemed to be so in love with Him. I wanted to know Him too and would imitate her actions in many ways.

Well, that journey took a side street as I reached my high school and college years. The foundation of the word was laid, but my desire to know Him was dim. I was still very active in the church and even joined my college gospel choir. But, my priority now was to fit in with the crowd, which did not include drawing closer to God. *"No man can come to me, except the Father which hath sent me draw him: and I will raise him up at the last day."* (John 6:44 KJV).

After graduating from college, I eventually landed a job as

an accountant in the Federal Government. I married my childhood sweetheart and soon after was blessed with a baby boy. My means of travel in Washington DC was the subway. I was on my way to work one morning and the normal way to travel was to transfer from one train line to another at the Metro Center Station. As I was standing on the crowded platform and I saw a man staring at me. I thought, "Out of all of these people in this station, why is that man looking at me?" He made me feel very uncomfortable. He was dressed in a dirty trench coat, his hair was sticking straight up on top of his head and his beard was bushy. As the train approached, I said, "Lord, Please don't let that man follow me on the train." I got on the train, found a seat and sure enough, the man came and sat beside me. My heart was about to jump out of my chest in fear. I looked straight ahead as if I did not see him looking at me. Then he began to speak to me. "Are you saved?" he said in a very loud voice. I felt like everybody's eyes on that train were on me. I blurted out, "No!" He asked me "Well, why not? " My reply was "Because, I don't want to be." Then the train arrived at the station where I would depart. I hopped off the train in lightning speed and walked quickly to my job location. As I walked, my mind relived everything that had just happened. I told that man "No, I was not saved." Had I been fooling myself all of these years? Wasn't a good job, marriage and a baby enough? Did I allow the church going and the doing of good deeds substitute for a true relationship with God that only comes by way of accepting Jesus as Savior and Lord?

What a wakeup call for me! As I reflect back on this experience, the strange metro station man, whom I sincerely believe was sent by God to me, was like a present day John the Baptist.

"As it is written in the prophets, Behold, I send my messenger before thy face, which shall prepare thy way before thee. The voice of one crying in the wilderness, Prepare ye the way of the Lord, make his paths straight. John did baptize in the wilderness, and preach the baptism of repentance for the remission of sins. And there went out unto him all the land of Judaea, and they of Jerusalem, and were all baptized of him in the river of Jordan, confessing their sins. And John was clothed with camel's hair, and with a girdle of a skin about his loins; and he did eat locusts and wild honey; And preached, saying, There cometh one mightier than I after me, the latchet of whose shoes I am not worthy to stoop down and unloose." (Mark 1: 2-7 KJV).

Shortly after the metro station experience, I began to attend a work place bible study group where I truly heard, understood and received the word of God for salvation. (Romans 10:9, 10) I repented of my sins, accepted Jesus Christ as my Savior and Lord and was baptized in the Holy Spirit that very day.

Another major life changing experience was with a group of newborn Christians whose heart's desire was to establish a relationship with our Lord. Excited about our new walk, we would meet at lunchtime in the basement room. After we had prayed, we sat quietly waiting to hear the Lord speak to us. As we listened for a few minutes in intense silence, I said, "Did you hear that?" Everyone looked at each other and said, "No, What did you hear? " I heard the voice of the Lord speak to me for the first time. The words I heard were "seek me." Just as David cried out to the Lord in Psalm 27 and heard His voice, so did I. Little did I know at that time those words would be the beginning of a life long journey and relationship with my Father.

My desire to know the Lord intimately increased immediately. I would spend hours fellowshipping with Him in prayer and waiting to hear His voice. A love for God and a passion to pray for others began to well up in me. During the same timeframe, the Spirit of God led me to become a member of H.J. Hines Ministries under the leadership of Apostle Hattie Joyce Hines, where I was taught on the many facets of prayer, and how to pray God's word. I continue to sit under her leadership and teachings of the unadulterated word of God as I develop in my prophetic ministry.

Learning to be led by and flow in the Spirit through prayer is a humbling experience. As I sought the Lord on the behalf of others, and myself God began to unveil my spiritual condition and carnal nature. It was as if I was being peeled like an onion. Layer by layer God started to reveal wrong mindsets, attitudes, pride, fears and anxieties and began to show me that sin is a hindrance to answered prayers. *"If I regard iniquity in my heart, the Lord will not hear me."* (Psalms 66: 18). I repented and my thoughts, life choices and actions began to change.

As I yielded to His correction and delivering power, I experienced God's love for people growing in my heart. With my focus on Him, distractions were removed. Through dreams and visions, God would reveal various spiritual and physical conditions of people. I was clearly hearing His directions on what and how to pray specifically. A freedom and boldness in prayer was released in me and through the power of God, many prayers have been answered. To God be the Glory!

As mentioned earlier in the chapter, these past life experiences I have shared are to encourage you to examine, diligently search and pursue the Lord. It is by no means saying that I have attained all there is to know about our Father.

As a matter of fact, writing this chapter has challenged me to break though some hindering mindsets and to simply trust and believe God. *"I can do all things through Christ which strengtheneth me."* (Philippians 4:13 KJV). I continue to be perfected by the Lord, as I am obedient to His desires and call. What a blessing it is to be loved so much.

The word seek is an action verb. It denotes continuous, progressive, never-ending movement. As we continue to seek the presence of the Lord, we are continuously being conformed transformed and conformed into His image. When we come closer to Him, he reveals who He is in us and through us. As you pray, open up to the freedom of His presence and allow Him to be mighty in your life.

Let Us Pray

Father God, we praise You and exalt Your Name. There is no one like You. We thank you Lord for giving us a heart to know You. We desire to seek your face and fellowship with You. Our eyes are on You. Reveal to us the secret and deep things of Your heart. Let our prayers be filled with the knowledge of Your will in all wisdom and spiritual understanding. We ask in Jesus Name, Amen

PROPHETESS PATRECEA J. LAMB

Patrecea J. Lamb was born in Norfolk, Virginia. She is the only child of William M. (deceased) and Hazel D. Johnson. She is an exhorter and edifier with a mission and voice to make known the heart of God to all. She is also a patented jewelry inventor (US D516, 460 S) and entrepreneur. Patrecea has a successful career in the Federal Government for over 33 years. She is currently an Accounting Branch Chief at the Department of Housing and Urban Development.

In 1984, Prophetess Lamb heard and answered the call of God on her life. She receives much of her prophetic foundation and development under the leadership of Apostle Hattie Joyce Hines of H.J. Hines Ministries. She currently serves as an intercessor, Aroma of Worship singer and a Young Warriors for Christ Ministry teacher.

Prophetess Lamb is a member of Mount Olive Baptist Church where she serves as the leader of God's Army in Prayer (GAP) intercessory ministry. Patrecea is also the President of I Can Productions, Inc. The home based business was established as a result of a jewelry design inspired by a God given dream. She is the wife of Deacon Stanley Lamb and the mother of two sons, Payton and Wynton.

CHAPTER 4

Seeking Him in a Fresh Place

Tears tracing the contour of my face cried out for solace
The bustling chaotic sounds filled the atmosphere around me
The drought in my belly hungered for His touch
My travail like a strummed guitar echoed in desperation
I pressed to find a new threshing floor perfumed with His scent
I pushed pass the normalcy of my prayer, my praise
and my worship
The familiar place was old and worn I could not
access Him here any longer
Seeking His voice, His warmth, His glory – I gave a new surrender
I did not care what they thought or how I looked…
I spiraled until there was no more me….until I was completely free
With eagle wings I embrace the wind and soared to higher heights
Now happily I dance upon fresh dew… *in His presence*

Remember the adage "Old habits are hard to break"? Well unfortunately, that's true for those who willingly remain fixated on keeping things as they are. Living life without a "press" to do something more is naturally and spiritually unhealthy. It's also true that some have no real emergence to change the familiar. We have legalized comfort zones that benefit us nothing and dare to change them.

It's a lethargic melody that silently rocks one to sleep; old habits dull the spirit. Yes, we're living in the end times. We are unsure of what the next headlines will be in these perilous times. There are wars, rumors of wars, catastrophic disasters, marriage, and families dismantling. The atmosphere is filled with distractions causing some to become desensitized, losing hope, and focus. Constantly embracing the issues around us without question or concern nor challenge has lulled many to sleep.

"Besides this you know what [a critical] hour this is, how it is high time now for you to wake up out of your sleep (rouse to reality)" (Romans 13:11 NIV).

Let me share this example, most mornings I found myself driving the same route to work. It was convenient with minimal driving time, access to popular eateries and fuel-efficient. I travelled the exact route so frequently that one day reaching my office I could not recall most of the trip. I'd become "numb," "unconscious" to the splendor of a new day, sounds and feel of the road. I took my morning cruise for granted with little expectation for something spectacular to happen! As long as I arrived on time pulled into my normal parking space and punched the clock by eight; I was fine.

In our spiritual seek for God using the same access style could minimize the intendancy of the visit. Allowing your environment to dictate the "how" and "when" to worship must change. "I'm upset with my husband and this always happens around my worship time! The dinner was delicious and plenteous, but I can't keep my eyes open for eight o'clock prayer. "God I'll be right back I can't wait to text this message." The normalcy of our everyday routines cannot be the "trigger" as we seek God's attention. Taking the same route may cause us to drive right pass what God is speaking and manifesting in signs, warnings, and miracles.

Our God is progressive, effervescent, and a living capable power! He's mindful to provide the upmost care in our relationship. His pursuit is fresh! We're never second best or the cheaper selection on the menu. His seek for us is liken unto a suitor with roses and Godiva chocolates. He's a perfect gentleman with open arms. *"Yes, I have loved you with an everlasting love"* (Jeremiah 31:3 AMP). He considers the weight and value of the relationship and what He can implement to make it richer. He sets a canopy demonstrating His love; the cool of a spring breeze; the Robin's song echoing right under our window and the rainbow that intrigues our senses.

The Spirit of the Lord is beckoning us all to a new place of worship! A fresh altar without the murmuring of the day and contaminates of past experience. The Spirit of the Lord is systematically changing our environment so we can present ourselves anew. The Spirit of the Lord weeps for the sound of His handmaidens and the travail of labor from the midwives asking, "Where are you my beloved?" We must initiate a new "seek" for God as He continues to woe us into His presence. The corner store mentality of just dropping by when we need something will no longer do.

There's urgency in the Earth setting forth a new demand for true worship and intercession. Our thirst for Him must supersede the pant of the deer desperate for a cool drink from the water brook (Psalm 42:1). Our passionate seek for God (radical, aggressive, unhindered, and determined); will summon His attention if we tarry. This means "real work" on a personal level to release new expressions of worship. He anticipates our longing for Him. He awaits our sweet embrace. His ear is bowed for the new song exuding from our spirit. He desires the aroma of our personal worship. He looks for uplifted hands and tears of adoration. He awaits our conversations. He desires a beckoning to the waltz - it's our time to lead. *"The hand of our God is upon all them for good who seek Him"* (Ezra 8:22b KJV).

My sisters, anything that hinders or robs our chance of being in sweet communion with the Father is a distraction. It's no secret that women are receptacles – wide receivers taking on much even when some of it's not ours. Our unique design enables us to juggle and our ability to get the job done is second to none. However, in this season we need to be very clear about our assignments. Our hands touch before our minds release us to the work. We embrace opportunities that are clearly earmarked for somebody else because we have the ability to do it. It's imperative that we orchestrate our time wisely. God needs us to be unshackled by the cares of the day and "FREE" to move in this season!

Go back to the drawing board. Erase anything that's a "Time Bandit" in your life, on task to steal your space, your mind, and your time! God is ready to download your next assignments. Get ready for local and international travel! He is ready to download fresh dew in your spirit. Get ready to impart and impact! He is ready to download fire and power. Get ready to change the atmosphere! Get ready to advance for the Kingdom! He is ready to send bold witness to release His glory! Get ready to speak a word to the nations! He is ready to release the secrets of heaven. Yes, our previous Father is waiting for you!

Women of God, we can no longer allow distractions in our lives! Our family, employment, finances, and friendships have distracted us; even we have played a part.

Distractions no matter where they originate from come to derail and weaken us. Far, too, much time has been lost because we fail to prioritize the "needs list." *"But seek (aim at and strive after) first of all (His way of doing and being right), and then all these things taken together will be given"* (Matthew 6:33 NIV). No more compromising – be on point with your worship. No more broken promises – be on point in your seek of God. No more tardy, late arrivals and no shows to the threshing floor. *"O come, let us worship and bow down, let us kneel before the Lord our Maker"* (Psalm 95:6 NIV).

My personal longing for God has shifted and my desperate cry stirs my spirit to push for access. I re-establish my time to intimately pursue Him. I hunger for His embrace, warmth and words that will heal my broken heart. I'm lost without Him and need His divine direction for my life. I confess and apologize for missing the mark when I felt His pull to the Throne Room. I cannot take the back burner approach to access Him when my very life depends on His breath. In order to recalibrate your seek for God, take an honest assessment of our worship. We give our employers our time, talent and energy – how much more should we give to Him who blesses us? *"Exalt the Lord our God and worship at his footstool"* (Psalm 99:5 NIV).

The Spirit of the Lord is calling us back to a place of worship. Whether, we like it or not He is removing the obstacles. He's silencing the telephone and erasing the text messages.

He's stripping away what we call important and "must do's" in this hour. He taken time to "white out" the friends list (this is not the season for everybody). He's fired the "hold ups" and distributed pink slips to the things He told you to get rid of. Yes, He is bringing correction so we are drawn back to enjoy fresh water. So don't' find it strange to be alone in this season; longing for conversations you'll never have. Don't be surprised when the cell phone hardly rings. Don't be surprised if you sit alone for lunch at Applebees. Don't be too shaken up when all you have is "time" designated to be in His presence. Be overcome with joy knowing God has selected you to be a glory container in this season. *"But without faith it is impossible to please and be satisfactory to Him. For whoever would come near to God must [necessarily] believe that God exist and that He is the "rewarder" of those who "earnestly" and "diligently" seek Him [out]"* (Hebrews 11:6 KJV).

Women of God, it's time that we each evaluate our method of worship. We need to seriously consider implementing new idea's; fresh concepts for our next encounters with God. How much do you need Him? How hungry and thirsty are you for His direction? If you need to change the time of worship – do it! If you need to rearrange your prayer closet – do it! If you need to perfume the atmosphere with myrrh – do it! Re-establish a pure seek for God – push to birth a new tabernacle with Him. Be steadfast and diligent as you demonstrate your serious intention to gain His attention. Don't let "Time Bandits" rudely interrupt this refurbished place of worship. *"...let us strip off and throw aside every weight and that sin (distraction from people, place or things) which so readily (deftly and cleverly) clings and entangles us"* (Hebrews 12:1 NLT).

Arise with a new purpose in your heart to touch Him.

Arise with new zeal in your spirit to seek Him.

Arise with a new energy in your soul to express your love to Him.

My sister's, let's establish a new declaration and decree in the name of Jesus!

I will seek His glory anew and blow His mind when I show up! I will give Him praise for His loving kindness is more than life. No longer will I entertain what is spiritually unprofitable. No longer will I allow obstacles to rearrange my time. No longer will I allow anything to dictate how I access the Throne Room. No longer will I allow my schedule to minimize my "seek, my hunger, my thirst."No longer will I perfume my time with fatigue and excuses. No longer categorized as "MIA (Missing in Action), no show or late. I'm seeking God because of His love, mercy and care for who I am in Him! I press behind the veil to my miracle make and burden bearer. I press behind the veil to the one who knows the number of tears I've shed. I press behind the veil to experience the aroma of heaven, which heals my broken spirit. I seek Him with my whole heart; desperate for His touch and longing for His voice of comfort. I press behind the veil to the lover of my soul and lifter of my head.

My Precious Father,

I pray in the name of Jesus as you are drawing Kingdom daughters for end time assignments that we would solidify our posture of worship. Give us the power to dismantle every desire and issue that may cause our foot to slip and our efforts hindered. Uphold us in your right hand and steady us for the journey ahead. Empower and cover us afresh with the blood of Jesus the Christ our King and Governor. I thank you in advance for testimonies of refreshing times in your presence from my beloved sisters. I thank you now for strengthening us to stand, to declare, to orchestrate, to impart and to impact.

I thank you precious Father for the ability to seek your face and freely dance in your presence. I love you with an endless love and thankful you are my Father who keeps me, holds me and adores me. In the name and power of the Anointed One Jesus the Christ I pray – Amen

Now it's your time to lead!

PASTOR LINDA HARVEY

Pastor Linda Harvey is the Visionary and Founder for Fragrance of Faith Ministry in Pikesville, Maryland. She is a published poet, songwriter and contributor for SOAR Magazine. Reverend Harvey is a Maryland licensed mentor, domestic violence educator and advocate for human trafficking. Reverend Harvey is the recipient of numerous professional, ministry and community awards. Her greatest accomplishment is a beautiful daughter who is a ballerina, honor student and model.

CHAPTER 5

Know Him

People pray for many reasons. We may seek God to change things for us or for someone else. Other times when we pray, we are seeking God for something in particular – perhaps a new home, car, or something else that we desire. There are also many types of prayers. There are prayers of worship, praise, and thanksgiving. Then there are those prayers where we put up requests before God. Regardless of what we are praying for, or what type of prayer we are praying, we are required to seek Him. This search for God can become complicated when one does not know Him. This is a process that requires serious effort by the one seeking God. This seeking to know God comes through spending time with Him studying His word.

When newborn babies want something, they send off signals. They may cry when they are hungry, scream when they hurt, swing their arms when they are upset or move anxiously when they are tired. A loving parent observes, is in tune with, and responds to their children, making sure their needs are met. As children grow and enter school, verbal communication skills improve. It is then when they desire certain things from their parents that they are required to communicate beyond a cry, a scream, or an anxious movement.

Throughout my childhood, my parents, family, and teachers taught me to "ask" and to remember to say "please." If I really wanted something, I had to get this right. If my desire was granted, I was required to respond with a pleasant "thank you."

Once children become a little more independent and get this simple method down pat, most of the time and without warning, all of a sudden, the rules change. The standard is raised for getting a request granted and there is no guarantee that the parent will even hear the child's request. At this point in children's lives, the dynamics of the relationship with their parents change. Parent's expectations of their children are greater because children are able to do more for themselves and they can also think more logically. A child may ask their parents, "What's going on?" or they may say, "I thought you loved me!" A parent may hear, "Why can't you just give me what I want?"

In comparison to our spiritual birth, we, too, experience these types of growing pains. When babies are born, they enter the world seeing and adjusting to light for the first time. When we are born again (John 3:7), we must adjust to the light of our new life in Christ. We desire the sincere milk of the word so we are able to grow (I Peter 2:2). Our need for nurturing, guidance and attention is high and we ask a whole lot of questions. Our faith is at an all-time high because we are more willing to take God at His word. As we exercise our faith and demonstrate confidence, temptations and trials show up. Our requests seem to go unanswered and frustration may set in because everything changes. You may have wondered if God even cares, does He listen, or why can't He just give you what you want.

Often we are tempted to throw child-like temper tantrums in an effort to get God's attention. This is all, in the natural and the spiritual, a necessary transition in life. Just as growing children must seek out different avenues of approach that will get them what they desire from their parents, we (as children of God) must do the same thing with our Heavenly Father. This information does not come by being frustrated all the time when things don't seem to go your way. Nor does it come by running away from the search and talking negative about what is annoying you. Do not believe for one moment that kicking, screaming, whining, pouting and complaining are the answers and will bring about positive results. These types of behaviors only create a chaotic atmosphere for you and for anyone else who is actually paying any attention to you. Just as a child's temper tantrum exacerbates a parent's patience, so do our frustrated methods of reaching God cause our prayers to go unanswered. We must seek to know our Father so we can effectively pray to Him and get the result we desire from Him.

God is not a magician or a fairy tale character; nor is He a statue that you rub for good luck. He is not unreachable, untouchable, or unapproachable. Examine the Bible and seek out where to find God and how you should approach Him. Find out what He likes and what He hates. Look for what draws Him, what moves Him, and what pushes Him away. We must seek Him out and get to know Him. This forms a binding relationship with Him. If you do not know Him, then you cannot have a relationship with Him. This search can be as simple as spending quiet time sitting before God. At other times, you may lay before God, pouring your heart out to Him and allowing Him to fill you up with what you need. You may hear of others who get alone with God and dance until they can dance no more – praising God and, at the same time, being released from anything that was keeping them bound. You must diligently seek Him by faith (Hebrews 11:6), so you can know God and get results in prayer. Just as you would no more go to hear a famous author and participate in a conversation regarding his or her material without reading it before you arrive, you should not expect to come before an Almighty God without first reading His book. Take a moment to test your knowledge of the One who holds the answers to our prayers. Ask yourself the following questions:

- What is the Lord's delight?

- What is God to those who diligently seek him?

- If you seek the Lord early, what is His promise to you?

- What six things does the Lord hate?

- What does the Lord require of you?

If you did not know the answer to at least one of these questions, seek the Lord. If you answered all of the questions correctly, there is so much more to God--keep seeking Him. The answers to these questions can be found in Proverbs 15:8, Hebrews 11:6, Proverbs 8:17, Proverbs 6:16-21 and Deuteronomy 10:12. It is absolutely necessary to KNOW our heavenly Father. He is our source, provider, comforter, healer … within Him is embodied all we need.

The indwelling of the Holy Spirit is our connection with our Heavenly Father. In John Chapter 14 (KJV), Jesus said some important words before He left to go back to the Father. In verse one, He said, *"Let not your heart be troubled: ye believe in God, believe also in me."* He goes on to say in verses 6 and 7, *"I am the way, the truth, and the life: no man cometh unto the Father, but by me. If ye had known me, ye should have known my Father also: and from henceforth ye know him, and have seen him."* Then in verses 12 through 18, *"Verily, verily, I say unto you, He that believeth on me, the works that I do shall he do also; and greater works than these shall he do; because I go unto my Father. And whatsoever ye shall ask in my name, that will I do, that the Father may be glorified in the Son. If ye shall ask any thing in my name, I will do it. If ye love me, keep my commandments. And I will pray the Father, and he shall give you another Comforter, that he may abide with you forever; even the Spirit of truth; whom the world cannot receive, because it seeth him not, neither knoweth him: but ye know him; for he dwelleth with you, and shall be in you. I will not leave you comfortless: I will come to you."*

Finally, in verses 26 and 27, He says, *"But the Comforter, which is the Holy Ghost, whom the Father will send in my name, he shall teach you all things, and bring all things to your remembrance, whatsoever I have said unto you. Peace I leave with you, my peace I give unto you: not as the world giveth, give I unto you. Let not your heart be troubled, neither let it be afraid."* God is not trying to hide from us nor withhold good from us (Psalm 84:11). He longs for our seeking Him in prayer; however, it can only be effective if we know Him.

A sign of someone who knows God is one who keeps His commandments (I John 2:3). The rewards are great and your prayer life will be effective, especially when you know that *"all the promises of God in him are yea, and in him Amen*" (II Corinthians 1:20 KJV).

You understand that after you pray for something, you confidently and patiently wait for the manifestation. There is no need to worry or fret. There is no reason to doubt and live in unbelief. His perfect loves casts out all fear (I John 4:18), but you must have that relationship to experience this perfect love. God loves you so much that when you do not know how you ought to pray, the Spirit intercedes for you (Romans 8:26).

How well do you know the only one who answers your prayers? How much time do you spend searching for God? It's not enough to know about Him, you must know Him for yourself or your prayers may go unanswered. Jesus was tempted in all points just as we are (Hebrews 4:15). At one point, in Luke 22:43-44, Jesus struggled in prayer. He knew the Father and understood what He was sent to accomplish. He was able to continue to move forward full of peace and with a matchless confidence. The world did not understand Him. He could have called heaven down to wipe out the entire planet, but this was not what the Father sent Him here to do – and He knew this.

In my own personal quest to find God, I studied the word all the time. I found out, as Hebrews 4:12 states that "*the word of God is quick, and powerful, and sharper than any two-edged sword*" (KJV). I sought out the names of God and I had dictionaries in my library to clarify what I was finding out. Early in my ministry, there were no computers, internet or online Bibles to pull information. Before the technology that exists today, there were reference books, pens and paper. My search was not based on other's opinions; it was based on what was before me in the word of God. All I was taught by preach ers and teachers had to line up with the word. My search for God was not based on how well I knew the one delivering the word, but it was based on my knowledge of God.

I have made many wrong turns in life. As I sought God for help, I already knew not to blame Him. I already knew that He gives us free will and does not force Himself on us. I also knew that He promised never to leave me, nor forsake me. I knew that He was my refuge and strength. He was a present help in trouble (Psalm 46:1). This knowledge made my search for answers more resolved and helped bring me out.

My sincere prayer for you today is that you know God. In knowing Him, your search for Him will bring about life-changing results and help your prayer life to be more effective. Please know that God promised in Matthew 7:8: *"For every one that asketh receiveth; and he that seeketh findeth; and to him that knocketh it shall be opened"* (KJV). Remember that knowing and seeking God is a process. We all start out as babes and grow as we continually study the word of God.

Prayer

Father, in the name of Jesus, we come boldly before Your throne of grace, that we may receive mercy and find grace to help in our time of need. We desire to seek your face and to know You for who You are. We know that You hear and answer prayers. Help us to relentlessly pursue You, God. In our search for You, let our prayer lives ascend to heights beyond our imagination. Quicken our spirits, rejuvenate our minds and let us not be the same. Thank you! We count in done in Jesus' Name. Amen.

BARBARA SILVER SMITH

Barbara Silver Smith was born and raised in Fredericksburg, Virginia. She is the daughter of Mother Lillie Silver and the late Elder Raymond Silver. Throughout the years, Evangelist Barbara has served in many capacities within ministry, including teacher, prayer intercessor, choir director, playwright, praise and worship leader, and youth leader. She has been an evangelist for over 20 years and now pastors Kingdom Community Outreach Ministries, currently headquartered in Blackstone, Virginia, alongside her husband, Pastor Ronnie T. Smith, Sr., to whom she has been married for seven years. Together, they have seven children. In addition to her Pastoral duties, she is an anointed singer, songwriter, and playwright.

In 2012, she received her Bachelor's of Science degree in Psychology, with a Minor in Christian Counseling, and a Specialization in Life Coaching, from Liberty University. She is currently pursuing her Master's degree in Counseling. Evangelist Barbara is the C.E.O. of Silver Smith & Associates, a firm dedicated to presenting professional seminars empowering women. Her specialty is conducting seminars on the benefits of laughter. She also serves as a volunteer with the Virginia Army National Guard and a number of other local organizations.

CHAPTER 6

Do You Really Trust Me (God)?

Dear reader, I pray as I inscribe what I hear from the Holy Spirit to share will be a blessing to you and that you trust God even more like never before. Never stop seeking the face of the Father because He has all your answers to your prayers. *"But as for me, I trust in You, O Lord. I say, "You are my God."* (Psalm 31:14 New Life Version NLV).

I guess you are wondering what is this author talking about, "Do You Really Trust God"? Well, it is not the title I came up with, but it is what the Holy Spirit gave me for this chapter. Let us discover why. God was saying to me as it relates to the word "seek," from Matthew 7:7-8 (NKJV), *"Ask, and it will be given to you; seek, and you will find; knock, and it will be opened to you. For everyone who asks receives, and he who seeks finds, and to him who knocks it will be opened."* He was saying to me that the word "seek[15]" - which means: 1: to resort to: go to; 2 *a*: to go in search of: look for *b*: to try to discover; 3: to ask for: request <*seeks* advice> 4: to try to acquire or gain: aim at <*seek* fame>; 5: to make an attempt – is an action word meaning it requires you to do something, requiring you to get involved.

Seeking God requires that you position yourself to hear God.

To seek the Lord is to know He has the answer that you are seeking. *"We are sure that if we ask anything that He wants us to have, He will hear us. If we are sure He hears us when we ask, we can be sure He will give us what we ask for."* (I John 5:14-15 NLV). If you know the answer to your problem or situation, you would not need to seek the Father.

Trusting God is to know you are not all knowing, but God is omniscient, which means He is all- knowing. *"You know when I sit down and when I get up. You know my thoughts before I think them. You know where I go and where I lie down. You know everything I do. LORD, even before I say a word, you already know it. You are all around me—in front and in back— and have put your hand on me. Your knowledge is amazing to me; it is more than I can understand."* (Psalm 139:2-6 New Century Version NCV).

I know you are probably saying I know this. If we know, why is it that we do not trust Him earnestly? Instead, we trust others for answers concerning our situation more than God. Trusting God involves having a relationship with God. We know a relationship is between two people. However, in order to have a relationship you must get to know the other person personally and that is how it should be with God the Father. We must get to know Him personally by spending more quiet time with Him in His word instead of more time with others, so that we truly get to know our Father. When we get to know our Father more we can trust Him. Isn't that how it works in a physical relationship with someone? You get to know them personally, the things you like and don't like about the person. You find out their strengths and their weakness. You find out how they feel about you whether you're girlfriend or a boyfriend.

We spend a lot of time getting to know people, but not as much time to get to know God. As you get to know the person, you begin to trust the person because you know more about them, which makes you feel safe and secure to share your personal information. Yet we don't trust God enough with our problems. Now back to the title "Do You Really Trust Me (God)?

I hear the Father saying if you truly trust me why are you seeking others for the answers to your problems. That is not showing me that you trust. Trusting me is according to Proverbs 3:5-6, *"Trust in the Lord with all your heart, and do not trust in your own understanding. Agree with Him in all your ways, and He will make your paths straight." (NLV).*

I'm reminded of the way I had to trust God and seek Him. In doing so it helped me to learn more about my Father (God). Trusting and seeking my Father helped me to discover and to know Him as a healer. Let me share if you don't mind.

I have a son that will be 19 years old on May 31st and I truly praise God for his life and allowing him to share another year with my husband and me. When my son was at the tender age of 4 years old, his appendix ruptured. He was walking around in so much pain in his side. But, I knew yet God had his hands upon him.

I had to ask, seek, and knock at the throne of God in prayer during the time of my oldest son's appendix rupturing after the doctor told us he would not make it. I was also asking and seeking God to keep my son because the doctors' didn't know what was wrong with my son and the sharp pains in his side continued. For two weeks, two different doctors examined him and they could not tell us what was wrong.

They informed us that his bowels were backed up (please excuse the words I'm using), but I hope you get the understanding of what I'm talking about. I had to continue to seek the face of God through faith and trust towards the one who could see me through my time of tribulation. *"Now faith is being sure we will get what we hope for. It is being sure of what we cannot see."* (Hebrews 11:1 NLV).

I asked God to keep my son as the doctors were seeking to find out what was wrong with him. If I wasn't seeking the face of God and trusting him for answers, I would not have heard God tell me that my son was going to be alright. He told me I must trust in Him and believe in Him and my son would be healed – even when the doctor said he wouldn't make it. *"But Jesus beheld them, and said unto them, With men this is impossible; but with God all things are possible."* (Matthews 19:26 KJV).

The poison was going through his body because when his appendices ruptured he was vomiting up the poison. But, he is here today – Hallelujah! – as a miracle child. The doctors said he would not make it, but my God told me he would and to trust and have faith in Him. By seeking God and trusting Him, it put me in a position of knowing Him as a Jehovah Rapha "The One Who Heals." He healed my son. My son was hospitalized for 2½ weeks. That's how serious it was, but God. What would have happened if I did not ask, seek, and knock and position myself to hear? I probably would not have heard the voice of the Lord telling me that he would be okay and to have faith to trust HIM. This Christian life is a about relationship.

Now if I can continue to stress the importance of seeking God and trusting Him for the answers, knowing He will work it all out for the good. *"And we know that all things work together for good to*

those who love God, to those who are the called according to His pur
pose." (Romans 8:28 NKJV). Let me tell you of a mother's heartache,
knowing you raised your daughter to be the godly daughter the best
you could and to live a life as a godly mother and wife before her. Can
I tell you that shortly before her graduation in 2008, my daughter got
mixed up with the wrong crowd of young people and got involved in
a homosexual relationship? Several other things occurred that lead
her into this relationship that I will not document in this chapter in
respect for her privacy. However, I will tell you how it truly caused
heartache beyond words as a mother. It really had me thinking I
wasn't a good mother and that I did some wrong in raising my baby
girl. I asked God, what did I do wrong? I begin to seek Him to know
how to deal with her. She was in such a state of rebellion. She was
not listening to my husband or me. The wrong crowd had her ear
and attention. She left home prematurely; she was not ready for this
cruel world. I never imagined this happening to my daughter. It was
the last thought from my mind, but what God told me concerning
my daughter is – she has to walk out her own journey. She had to
find out things as it pertains to this world on her own. God promised
me that He would bring her out of this situation. He would deliver
her, but she had to go through it first. We never know how long deliverance for a love one will take no matter what type of deliverance
is needed. I promise you, if you trust God and let patience have its
perfect work. Manifestation will come at God's perfect timing. *"But
let patience have its perfect work, that you may be perfect and complete, lacking nothing."* (James 1:4 NKJV).

My position was to continue to seek the Father face for wisdom to know how to deal with my daughter because I didn't know

how to deal with it on my own. *"If any of you lacks wisdom, let him ask of God, who gives to all liberally and without reproach, and it will be given to him."* (James 1:5 NKJV). When I was seeking God, I was seeking for wisdom because I didn't know how to handle this situation. No one could tell me how to handle the situation with my daughter, but God. Why is that? In my eyes and what I told God when I was seeking Him is that you are the creator of all things. You created my daughter and me, you know me best, and you know her better than I do because you created her. She is your daughter first before she became my physical daughter. So, I entrust my daughter in your hands God because you gave her to me and you knew her before you placed her in my womb. *"Before I formed you in the womb I knew you…"* (Jeremiah 1:5 NKJV).

God instructed me to love her through this situation, but not to compromise my belief about homosexuality and fall into a trap of the enemy trying to make me think I would lose my daughter, if I were not in agreement with her decision or support it. *"Hate starts quarrels, but love covers every wrong."* (Proverbs 10:12 GOD'S Word GW). I had to show her sincere love and not hate that brings on arguments. When it comes to our children we tend to compromise or wavier when it comes to God's word of truth. This is because we think we will lose our children to the world, but we must trust God, follow the instructions He gives us through seeking His face, and trust what we heard Him tell us to do. It really hurt my heart so badly to see my daughter go through 3 years of this relationship. There were many days of tears falling from my face, but the word of God says in *"Those who sow in tears Shall reap in joy."* (Psalm 126:5 NKJV).

I was waiting that special day to reap the joy of my tears I cried over my daughter's situation. Don't get me wrong I trusted God, but know we are still human and have feelings (emotions). However, my emotions didn't stop me from trusting God to deliver my daughter. On many occasions, she would come back home to live. I would let her know we love you and if you need to come home, you are welcome, but there is a standard in my house according to Joshua 24:15"… *But as for me and my house, we will" serve the LORD."* (NKJV). She would never stay longer than a few months when she did return home, but God kept me in tune to what was going on with her during this process of her journey. Never did God leave me or ignore what was going on. Why you ask? This was because I was still seeking Him to know how to continue to pray for my daughter for her deliverance to be manifested. I also went through a short period of being ashamed about my daughter's situation. Wondering what others thought about my daughter and me being a Minister of the Gospel of Jesus Christ. I had to learn not to be concerned about what other thought because we all have sinned according to Romans 3:23 *For all have sinned and fall short of the glory of God."* (NKJV). This was not my daughter's final destination. I could see God taking her through her healing process as she begin to talk with me about situations She could see I wasn't judging her for her sins. However, no matter what, I told her the truth of God's Word and let her know that I would not compromise. I can't compromise no matter what God made Adam (man) and Eve (woman) to cleave together (Genesis 2) and not man to man or woman to woman.

On Saturday, November 5, 2011, my daughter was delivered while attending a woman's conference titled" Are You Among the

Chosen" hosted by Overseer Trena Stephenson CEO/Founder of Woman of God Ministries. I invited my daughter to come because I was one of the speakers and she actually showed up, but I didn't expect her to, praise Jesus. The Woman of God called my daughter to the altar and spoke the word of Lord concerning her situation and that is when my daughter was delivered from the spirit of homosexuality. That is when my tears I had sewn had reaped in joy. That was truly a day of celebration because I knew her life would never be the same again. The power of darkness was lifted off her and she made a decision to turn from her wicked ways to turn back to the True Living God. As the title reads "Do You Really Trust Me (God)? I had to live it out by seeking and trusting Him every step of the way for 3 years to know Him as the God that delivers.

Father, in the name Jesus! I pray that my sister or my brother that has read this chapter was blessed by it. And that it shown them how important it is that when we seek you in prayer that we trust you to give us the answer and that you will never leave us or forsake us, but you are there to walk us through to see our prayers manifested. In Jesus Name I pray, Amen!

TAMMY L. MCNAIR

Pastor Tammy L McNair is an anointed, gifted, and compassionate preacher and teacher of the Gospel of Jesus Christ. She is CEO and Founder of Sister Circle Ministries Inc. in Waldorf, MD under the leadership and spiritual covering of Overseer Trena Stephenson, Woman of God Ministries Inc. Sister Circle Ministries is a women ministry of Sisters in Christ learning and growing together in Christ. Sisters receive healing, restoration, deliverance, and embracing their spiritual gift(s) and calling to impact the Kingdom of God. She is married to Keith R McNair Sr. of 19 years and has been blessed with three beautiful gifts from God: Vaneese, Keith Jr., and Joseph, and reside in Maryland. She stands in faith according to Matthew 19:26… "With God all things are possible."

Email: www.SisterCircle2003@aol.com
Web Site: www.SCMinistries04.com
Ministry Line: 240-346-0056

CHAPTER 7

*For the Father Seeketh,
Such to Worship Him*

*"God is a Spirit: and they that worship him must worship him in
spirit and in truth."* (John 4:24 KJV).

The understanding of the God's presence is more than just finding yourself a way out of hard times. It is to love him with all your heart and soul. The bible says, "God is a spirit," signifying His Omni-presences in the earth and heavens. This gives man the ability to have relationship with Him through meditation and spiritual intimacy. Finding yourself in the presence of God causes an awareness of the spirit and allows you to have strong sense of discernment concerning life's matter.

The word of God teaches us in the Gospel according to Saint John 4:23, *"But the hour cometh, and now is, when the true worshippers shall worship the Father in spirit and in truth: for the Father seeketh such to worship him."* (KJV). Wow what an answer to all of our day-to-day, life issues.

After meeting a woman who was plagued with serious problems, most of us would have desired to keep to ourselves.

It was in her transparent place that, she received the greatest revelation for her life. Many times in life, it is the will of God for us to receive the answer to our circumstances, but the area that causes hindrance comes in our flesh when it desires to hide from the presence of God. Just for a moment, let's consider the story of Adam and God in the Garden. It begins in Genesis 2 after that God had fashioned Eve from Adams rib. Causing them to be one flesh, they were naked as it states in verse 25 ;*"And they were both naked, the man and his wife, and were not ashamed."* (Genesis 2:25 KJV) .

The transition comes in the next chapter, after Eve is deceived and Adam allows himself to follow. *"And they heard the voice of the LORD God walking in the garden in the cool of the day: and Adam and his wife hid themselves from the presence of the LORD God amongst the trees of the garden." "And the LORD God called unto Adam, and said unto him, where art thou?" "And he said , I heard thy voice in the garden, and I was afraid , because I was naked; and I hid myself."* (Genesis 3:8-10 KJV). Can we take just a moment to think what actually happened here. I call it the "Great Disconnect," this story constitutes to man the action of the serpent Satan and his true character. This disconnect was designed by Satan to cause man to be disabled from the presence of God. What happens now is that you become disconnected from the source of power or in my own word the source of life?

There is an immediate break down in the ability to communicate. As believers, we must have clear communication with the power source. Who is our power source? God is our power source. Yes, He who created all things gives man the strength to live. The plan of God was for His master creation "man" to have all things per taining to happiness, health, and holistic life. Let's look a little closer at the story in Genesis. God created the garden, in that garden He provided everything that Adam and Eve needed to live in his divine splendor. There was no need for Adam to have to believe because he *had dominion* over all that was made.

Adam was God's voice upon the earth, so all things made by God responded to the voice that *had dominion* over them. The word dominion is defined as to have control or the exercise of control or sovereignty. One who rules over a territory or sphere of influence, control; one who has mastering of a realm. Adam's voice had power as long as he remained in the presence of God. As believers, we must remain in the posture to communicate with God. Adam's posture because of his state of disobedience, caused him to reframe from communicating with God as he had been instructed. Disobedience will cause you to hide yourself from God. The scripture say that Adam and Eve hid themselves. Why you ask? After they had eaten or partaken of "the tree of knowledge of good and evil" this caused a state of disobedience because it was forbidden to them to eat from that tree. One of the most important revelations I ever received from God, it is a simple statement, but it rings with great truth "the Blessed is On the Instruction." A person who receives instruction is less likely to error in direction and they are more careful to follow after correction. Instruction leads you to follow a path of wisdom. It was not wise of Adam to follow Eve, because God never give the instruction to Eve. The instruction was given to Adam and so was the dominion over all things given to Adam. For this reason, Adam lost his posture to remain in God's presence. Disobedience causes disconnection. God created man to have fellowship with him.

It is the will of God for man to follow as His instructions. Man is led by the spirit." *And the LORD God formed man of the dust of the ground, and breathed into his nostrils the breath of life; and man became a living soul."* (Genesis 2:7 KJV). After the receiving of life, the instant man breathed he became God driven. True life is only found when you have fellowship with the source of life. As believers, we must maintain and continue fellowship with God through regular worship practices. Worship is the consistent component that allows kingdom citizens to have fellowship with God and their fellow man. Fellowship is a form of communicating with God by a spiritual means. Worship is the greatest element of communication between God and man, it allows man to have intimacy with God.
"God is a Spirit: and they that worship him must worship him in spirit and in truth." (John 4:24 KJV).

Here is the answer to the issue of communication between God and man. The writer John says it so wonderfully. God is a Spirit. When man was form, the spirit of God was released in him through the breath of God. So just so God is a spirit, man has a part of Him, which is also spirit. The spirit of man allows him to fellowship with God by worship. There are various forms of worship.

1. Adoration -the act of paying honor, as to a divine being; worship. reverent homage. fervent and devoted <u>love</u>.

2. Exaltation- / the act of <u>exalting</u>. the state of being <u>exalted</u>.

3. Meditation-the act of <u>meditating.</u> continued or extended thought; reflection; contemplation. <u>transcendental meditation.</u> devout religious contemplation or spiritual introspection.

4. Daily devotion by studying of the Scripture. Reading the bible on a daily basis and the study of the bible.

5. Praise- the act of expressing approval or admiration; commendation; laudation. the offering of grateful homage in words or song, as an act of worship: the state of being approved or admired.

6. Prayer- to offer thanksgiving in a form of sacred request, a way of communication through spiritual meditation and confession to God.

7. Seeking- To endeavor to obtain or reach, To go to or toward, To inquire for; or request.

The Spirit of God gives believers access to His presence. The above methods are used as ways to creating intimacy with God. When we as followers of Christ choose to commune with God, it causes an awareness of matter of life. Faith is developed when we as believers fellowship or commune with God on a consistent schedule. The practice of regular worship opens the eyes of our understanding to the word of God and the manifestation of kingdom principles on the earth.

All of the above methods can be accomplished through believers learning how to "seek" the Father. *"For the Father seeketh such to worship him.*" (John 4:23 KJV). God, the Father, desires that man would be in a constant state of communication with Him. It is the Father's wish that believers would live a life of worship. Living a life of worship develops spiritual intimacy. It is in the intimacy with God that you learn His ways and His character. When we as followers of Christ learn His ways, this gives us power to overcome the obstacles of this world and walk in a perpetual state of victory.

As believers, we must declare the name of the Lord. His name is, His character. The Hebrew word for name refers to more than the sound that is made with your lips. It identifies one's reputation and character. I like to use the word attribute. When we seek God, it opens our mind to the power of His name. Many times people will try to invoke the spirit of God in worship experiences. God's presence doesn't have to be invoked when believers seek after His presence.

Seeking the presence of God causes demonstration in the spirit realm. The bible teaches this in the book of the Gospel according to St. Luke through a woman who had an issue of bleeding, or an infirmity in her body. She suffered with this sickness for twelve years. Trying to solve her problem, she sought out many physicians, and none had the ability to cure the sickness that plagued her. The bible tells us that she heard about a healer, His name was Jesus and that He was able to cure her of this longtime sickness. So, she pressed her way to get close to Him. Stop for a moment, the word pressed signifies that there was some effort to get to Jesus. Yes, we as believers must have such an overwhelming desire to be where God is, sometime we must exercise this in the spirit. This is to seek Him through prayer, fasting, and all other forms of spiritual intimacy. I believe that the woman sought after the savior. It was only when she get in His presence that she received her healing. She said these words *"If I can but touch the hem of His garment, I know that I shall be made whole."* (Mark 5:28 KJV). As followers of Christ, we must trust in the power of His presence. Seeking the presence of God creates the atmosphere for miracles. Though, we shall not just seek after the presence of God just to receive from Him, these are part of the benefits that come from walking close with God.

God is a spirit and they that worship must worship in Spirit and in Truth. As believers, worship should be a regular part of our daily activities. The most perfected way to commune with God is through worship. Worship is the act of entering into divine presence by spiritual meditation, adoration, exaltation, or praise. Worship creates an open door to the supernatural by mediation of the spirit. Seeking God is the most important; it allows man to enter into a great form of intimacy. God is a spirit, because of this the only way to fellowship with God in by the spirit of truth. The spirit of truth causes believers to be aware of their shortcomings and faults that might hinder any open area of communication with God.

God is the spirit of truth. He is the light of the world. Light exposes and reveals what may be covered in a dark place. As a seeker, you must walk in truth allowing the Holy One to cover areas that may be closed because of unbelief, bitterness, hurt, unforgiveness, or any other sin that can stand between man and God. See as it was previously stated man was created to live in the presence or fellowship of God. Only after sin or disobedience took place did man lose his divine ability to walk with God in the garden.

In the Gospel of St. John, Christ opens the door to man that he might re-enter into his rightful divine place in God's presence. When we seek God, it allows a spiritual awakening where we as believers are able to walk in the spirit of manifestation by the succession of our forefathers. This is an inheritance that comes to believers through spiritual access. The bible says and He gave Peter the keys to the kingdom, what we bind on earth shall be bound in heaven, and what we loose on earth shall be loosed in heaven. This represents our ability to move in the spirit by means of access to God's kingdom. Seeking God gives us spiritual keys to open doors that have been closed in our lives.

The spirit of truth will bring all things to our understanding. Seeking the presence of God allows believers to walk in a state of revelation. Not just having the logos of God, but His rhema word. Seeking, is one form of intimacy that causes believers in see into what God has designed for them to overcome the snare of the enemy and to be great conquers. The word of God declares that we are more than conquers. As believers, there is no problem, circumstance, or situation that God cannot allow us to be aware of and have to ability to overcome it. In the words of a great theologian, seeking God is a gift "no struggle." No struggle in our finances. No struggle in our homes. No struggle in our ministries. No struggle in whom God has called us to be. No struggle in the next dimension of our lives.

Beloved, if you would pray this prayer of seeking power. Father thank You for an open door to come before you. I praise You for Your son Jesus who has made the way easy for me to enter into your presence. As a believer, I come asking that You would help me to walk in the spirit of truth. Allowing You to lead and guide me. Thank

You that there is nothing that by Your spirit cannot be open unto me. I trust You and will follow Your word as it is written in St. John 4. Thank You that my desire is to walk with You in the spirit. Father I ask that You would cause everything that is not like You to be revealed to me. And now I repeat, I ask You the forgive me. Thank You Heavenly Father that because of Jesus I live in Your spirit and receive Your voice. I seek after Your righteousness and receive the fullness thereof. God there is no place or circumstance that I am confronted with that You have not already given me victory over. Thank You God that there is no struggle, because of You. I believe and I receive thy kingdom come and thy will be done. In Jesus Name and It is so. So be it.

Once you have prayed this prayer, be sure to wait for the voice of God to speak to you in the spirit. Beloved He will come, if you ask him. Seek Him while He may be found.

CHIEF APOSTLE WILLIAM BILLUPS

Born to Elder Patricia and William V. Billups on March 24, 1980 this gift to the body of Christ survived death before he could fight for himself. Doctors gave Patricia little hope for this baby born with a heart condition. God had a plan for his life even in that stage of his life. William survived, and the story of his anointed life continued. At the early age of five, the family saw the gifting of God on his life. William was raised in the Church of God in Christ. The call of God was evident on the life of Apostle Billups at a young age, by his singing in the choir. God later anointed him to play the organ and direct the choir. He began preaching at youth day services and revivals all over the Virginia. At the age of fourteen, Apostle Billups was licensed to preach the gospel under the Leadership of Rev. C.L. Myrick and the National Baptist Convention. He served as Youth Minister until he was released to help establish a new ministry at Mount Sinai Church of God with Pastor Arthur Clark.

After hearing the clarion call of God to his church, he was consecrated to the Episcopal office of Bishop under the leadership of Chief Apostle J. Shawn Urquhart, Apostolic Fellowship of Churches, Inc.

Later he was installed as Chief Apostle and Presiding Prelate of Manifest Kingdom Fellowship Inc., by the College of Bishops.

Presently he serves as the Chief Apostle and Presiding Prelate of Manifest Kingdom Fellowship Worldwide and Global Alliances Inc. and Spiritual Advisor to the Prelate of Latter House Fellowship of Churches Ministries Inc., Baltimore MD. God has given him an awesome vision and a great people to carry it out. His accomplishments include an Associate's degree in Biblical Studies from Virginia Lynchburg Seminary and College, Certified Clinical Pastoral Education Certificate, and numerous other completions. Present, he is actively pursuing a Bachelor's degree in Business Administration. Bishop Billups was honored with an Honorary Doctorate of Divinity from the Wings of Faith Bible Institute.

Bishop Billups serves as the senior pastor and founder of New Vision Expansion Project of Manifest Kingdom "House of Levi Assembly" in the City of Hampton, Va. He is the husband of Overseer Felicia Billups. They are parents of five wonderful children and they oversee several pastors and churches nationwide. This dynamic man of God specializes in teaching and developing leaders, building churches and winning souls to Christ. As led by God, the Apostle travels all over the United States and eastern part of Canada preaching and teaching the message of empowerment to all who will listen. Get ready for a life-changing move as we say manifested in the words of the great hymn "You will never be the same again."

The Journey Through Prayer Begins

Well dear readers we are back again with a new series entitled "Seven Ingredients to an Effective Prayer Life." Through the reading of this book, you have discovered the first two ingredients must be effective in your life. The first ingredient is "humility." Some think that being humble means you are weak and easily intimated. But, I know that reading this book you found out that is not the case. In actuality you are strong, confident (In GOD), faithful and attentive. We have found out that humility is favorable in God's eyes and is a must to be successful in this Christian walk. Humility places you in position to be heard and be used by God. This leads me to the second ingredient, which is to "seek." Did you notice the order? One must be humble first postured correctly in order to seek God and be effective. I know you discovered how to properly seek the Father after you entered into the correct posture of humility. We found out we must seek God for all things not some things, but all things. I pray that as we continue this journey together that our faith will be renewed and our pray life will increase with passion and fire. There are five more ingredients to learn about in order to become completely effective in our pray life. This is an awesome journey we have embarked upon. I'll see you on our next stop of this journey.

I love you more than you will ever know.

Trena

VISIONARY

Overseer Trena Stephenson is a gifted preacher, teacher, worship leader, author, playwright, entrepreneur and intercessor. Overseer Trena developed and formed Daughters of Distinction, LLC in 2008, based off of her passion for writing and helping others fulfill their passions, as well.

Daughters of Distinction was designed to impact this world with the Gospel of Jesus Christ through books, TV and radio ventures. She is a visionary, a woman of great faith, compassion, and integrity. She has been the guest speaker on "The Wenda Royster Show," a radio broadcast of Radio One; Rejoice TV Network; TBN, and Preach the Word Network. In April 2008, Overseer Stephenson became the Executive Producer and Creative Director for Daughters of Distinction TV, which houses two television shows Daughters of Distinction Live and Let's Talk a new show that launched in April 2011. Both shows will air on Rejoice TV Network in MD and DC. In May 7, 2011, Overseer Stephenson launched The Fullness of God Radio Broadcast now airing in the states of AL, FL, GA, SC, NC, LA, and PA. In September 2011, Overseer Trena also launched Soar Magazine an online magazine to empower and encourage the people of God. When God opens the door for Overseer Stephenson, she walks through it under the Anointing of the Holy Spirit with the purpose of leading someone to Christ.

To learn more about this awesome woman of God, you can log onto www.dofdllc.com.

7 INGREDIENTS TO AN EFFECTIVE PRAYER LIFE
VOLUME 3 -5

Due to Release Decemeber 8, 2012

RELEASES FROM DAUGHTERS OF DISTINCTION
Introducing the Series Entitled "The Fullness of God"

And He Still
Hears

And He Still
Speaks

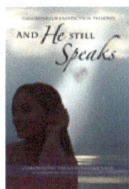

And He Still
Sees

And He Still
Waits

Woman of God Ministries Inc. Presents

The Fullness of God Broadcast

ON AIR

WUD AM 1270 (Mobile, AL) Saturdays 1:30 PM - 2:00 PM
WFAM AM 1050 (Augusta, GA & Aiken, SC) Saturdays 3:30 PM - 4:00 PM
WYYC AM 1250 (York-Harrisburgh, PA) Sundays 5:00 PM -5:30 PM
WTJ (Pensacola, FL) Saturdays 7:00 AM - 7:30 AM
KIOU (Shreveport, LA) Fridays 7:00 PM - 7:30 PM
WSKY (Asheville, NC) Fridays 7:30 PM - 8:00 PM

Beginning in July every 2nd Thursday at 7:30 PM is a time to hear
from our listeners with prayer requests, questions and testimonies.
Conference Dial-in Number: (712) 775-7000
Participant Access Code: 759489#

Overseer Trena Stephenson
Host & Founder
www.wofgod.org

Co-Host Minister Renatta Jones-Brice
Just Blessed Enterprises
www.facebook.com/jonesbrice1

Co-Host Prophetess Mia McGee
of W.A.V.E Ministries
www.waveministries.com

To learn more about the services and upcoming releases go to
www.dofdllc.com
Find us on the web @ www. soarmagazine.info &
www.wofgod.org

REFERENCES

1. Hawks, Annie. "I Need Thee Every Hour." Christian Music Publishing, 1872
2. Caesar ,Shirley. "Yes Lord, Yes." *Live...In Chicago*. World Records Production Company, 1988.
3. "Humility." *Dictionary.com Unabridged*. 1 March 2012 <http://dictionary.reference.com/browse/humility>
4. Murray, Andrew. "Humility." *World Invisible*. Accessed 1 March 2012. < <http://www.worldinvisible.com/library/murray/5f00.0565/5f00.0565.c.htm
5. Smith, Fred. "Christian Humility." *Christianity Today*. 2012. Accessed 1 March 2012 <http://www.ctlibrary.com/le/1984/winter/84l1118.html>
6. Living Word Church. "God Resists the Proud but Gives Grace to the Humble." *Now Faith.com*. March 13, 2012. Accessed 13 March 2012. <http://www.nowfaith.com/God%20Resists%20The%20Proud%20But%20Gives%20Grace%20To%20The%20Humble.pdf / >.
7. Dwyer, Devin. "Fact Check-Obama and Equal Pay for Women." *Political Punch*. ABC News, 01 31 2012. Web. 29022012. <http://abcnews.go.com/blogs/politics/2012/01/fact-check-obama-and-equal-pay-for women/>.
8. The Amplified Bible says in Matthew 5:3 that blessed (happy, [a]to be envied, and [b]spiritually prosperous--[c]with life-joy and satisfaction in God's favor and salvation, regardless of their outward conditions) are the poor in spirit (the humble, who rate themselves insignificant), for theirs is the kingdom of heaven! [a] Matthew 5:3 Alexander Souter, Pocket Lexicon of the Greek New Testament. [b] Matthew 5:3 Marvin Vincent, Word Studies. [c] Matthew 5:3 Hermann Cremer, Biblico-Theological Lexicon.
9. Murray, Andrew. "Humility." *World Invisible*. March 1, 2012. < http://www.worldinvisible.com/library/murray/5f00.0565/5f00.0565.c.htm
10. Loss, Myron. "Humility." *SermonCentral.com*. March 12, 2012. < http://www.sermoncentral.com/sermons/humility-myron-loss-sermon-on-growth-in-christ-66564.asp->
11. Murray, Andrew. "Humility." *World Invisible*. March 1, 2012. < http://www.worldinvisible.com/library/murray/5f00.0565/5f00.0565.c.htm
12. Loss, Myron. "Humility." *SermonCentral.com*. March 12, 2012. < http://www.sermoncentral.com/sermons/humility-myron-loss-sermon-on-growth-in-christ-66564.asp->
13. "seek." *Dictionary.com Unabridged*. Random House, Inc. 28 June. 2011. <Dictionary.com   http://dictionary.reference.com/browse/seek>.
14. seek." *Roget's 21st Century Thesaurus, Third Edition*. Philip Lief Group 2009. 09 Mar. 2012. <Thesaurus.com http://thesaurus.com/browse/seek>.
15. "seek." *Merriam Webster.com*. Merriam-Webster. 7 March. 2012. <http://www.merriam-webster.com/dictionary/seek>

The Prophetic Intercessors Council of an Empowered People (PICEP)
East Coast Region - Maryland Chapter

Pray for an East Coast Awakening and Revival!

"Restore My Desire"

Haggai 2:7

"Seeking the Father through Prayer
for REVIVAL"

Become a Corporate River Site &
Experience Rivers of Revival!!!

For information on the coming
"RIVERS OF CORPORATE PRAYER REVIVALS"
Call (240)682-9665/2472